Editor

Cristina Krysinski, M. Ed.

Editor in Chief

Karen J. Goldfluss, M.S. Ed.

Creative Director

Sarah M. Fournier

Cover Artist

Barbara Lorseyedi

Art Coordinator

Renée Mc Elwee

Imaging

Amanda R. Harter

Publisher

Mary D. Smith, M.S. Ed.

For correlations to the Common Core State Standards, see page 109 of this book or visit *http://www.teachercreated.com/standards*.

Teacher Created Resources

6421 Industry Way
Westminster, CA 92683
www.teachercreated.com

ISBN: 978-1-4206-8249-6

© 2015 Teacher Created Resources
Made in U.S.A.

Table of Contents

Introduction

Twenty different texts from a variety of genres are included in this reading comprehension resource. These may include humor, fantasy, myth/legend, folktale, mystery, adventure, suspense, fairy tale, play, fable, science fiction, poetry, and informational/nonfiction texts, such as a timetable, letter, report, procedure, poster, map, program, book cover, and cartoon.

Three levels of questions are used to indicate the reader's comprehension of each text.

One or more particular comprehension strategies have been chosen for practice with each text.

Each unit is five pages long and consists of the following resources and strategies:

- teacher information: includes the answer key and extension suggestions
- text page: text is presented on one full page
- activity page 1:   covers literal and inferential questions
- activity page 2:   covers applied questions
- applying strategies: focuses on a chosen comprehension strategy/strategies

Teacher Information

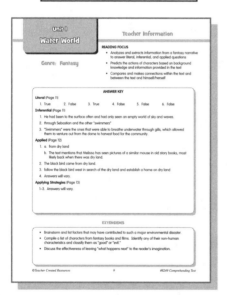

Text Page

- **Reading Focus** states the comprehension skill emphasis for the unit.
- **Genre** is clearly indicated.
- **Answer Key** is provided. For certain questions, answers will vary, but suggested answers are given.
- **Extension Activities** suggest other authors or book titles. Other literacy activities relating to the text are suggested.

- The title of the text is provided.
- Statement is included in regard to the genre.
- Text is presented on a full page.

Activity Page 1

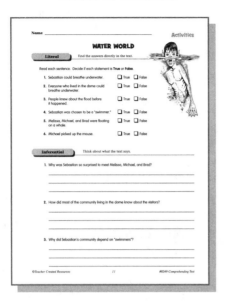

- **Literal** questions provide opportunities to practice locating answers in the text.
- **Inferential** questions provide opportunities to practice finding evidence in the text.

Activity Page 2

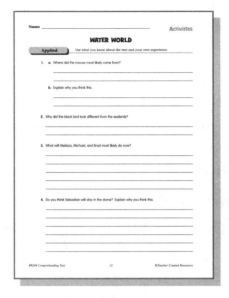

- **Applied** questions provide opportunities to practice applying prior knowledge.

Applying Strategies

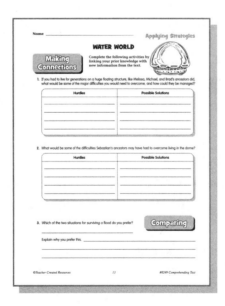

- Comprehension strategy focus is clearly labeled.
- Activities provide opportunities to utilize the particular strategy.

Types of Questions

Students are given **three types of questions** (all grouped accordingly) to assess their comprehension of a particular text in each genre:

- **Literal questions** are questions for which answers can be found directly in the text.

- **Inferential questions** are questions for which answers are implied in the text and require the reader to think a bit more deeply about what he or she has just read.

- **Applied questions** are questions that require the reader to think even further about the text and incorporate personal experiences and knowledge to answer them.

Answers for literal questions are always given and may be found on the Teacher Information pages. Answers for inferential questions are given when appropriate. Applied questions are best checked by the teacher following, or in conjunction with, a class discussion.

Comprehension Strategies

Several specific comprehension strategies have been selected for practice in this book.

Although specific examples have been selected, often other strategies, such as scanning, are used in conjunction with those indicated, even though they may not be stated. Rarely does a reader use only a single strategy to comprehend a text.

Strategy Definitions

Predicting	Prediction involves the students using illustrations, text, or background knowledge to help them construct meaning. Students might predict what texts could be about, what could happen, or how characters could act or react. Prediction may occur before, during, and after reading, and it can be adjusted during reading.
Making Connections	Students comprehend texts by linking their prior knowledge with the new information from the text. Students may make connections between the text and themselves, between the new text and other texts previously read, and between the text and real-world experiences.
Comparing	This strategy is closely linked to the strategy of making connections. Students make comparisons by thinking more specifically about the similarities and differences between the connections being made.
Sensory Imaging	Sensory imaging involves students utilizing all five senses to create mental images of passages in the text. Students also use their personal experiences to create these images. The images may help students make predictions, form conclusions, interpret information, and remember details.

Strategy Definitions (cont.)

Determining Importance/ Identifying Main Idea(s)

The strategy of determining importance is particularly helpful when students try to comprehend informational texts. It involves students determining the important theme or main idea of particular paragraphs or passages.

As students become effective readers, they will constantly ask themselves what is most important in a phrase, sentence, paragraph, chapter, or whole text. To determine importance, students will need to use a variety of information, such as the purpose for reading, their knowledge of the topic, background experiences and beliefs, and understanding of the text format.

Skimming

Skimming is the strategy of looking quickly through texts to gain a general impression or overview of the content. Readers often use this strategy to quickly assess whether a text, or part of it, will meet their purpose. Because this book deals predominantly with comprehension after reading, skimming has not been included as one of the major strategies.

Scanning

Scanning is the strategy of quickly locating specific details, such as dates, places, or names, or those parts of the text that support a particular point of view. Scanning is often used, but not specifically mentioned, when used in conjunction with other strategies.

Synthesizing/Sequencing

Synthesizing is the strategy that enables students to collate a range of information in relation to the text. Students recall information, order details, and piece information together to make sense of the text. Synthesizing/sequencing helps students to monitor their understanding. Synthesizing involves connecting, comparing, determining importance, posing questions, and creating images.

Summarizing/Paraphrasing

Summarizing involves the processes of recording key ideas, main points, or the most important information from a text. Summarizing or paraphrasing reduces a larger piece of text to the most important details.

Genre Definitions

Fiction and Poetry

Science Fiction These stories include backgrounds or plots based upon possible technology or inventions, experimental medicine, life in the future, environments drastically changed, alien races, space travel, genetic engineering, dimensional portals, or changed scientific principles. Science fiction encourages readers to suspend some of their disbelief and examine alternate possibilities.

Suspense Stories of suspense aim to make the reader feel fear, disgust, or uncertainty. Many suspense stories have become classics. These include *Frankenstein* by Mary Shelley, *Dracula* by Bram Stoker, and *Dr. Jekyll and Mr. Hyde* by Robert Louis Stevenson.

Mystery Stories from this genre focus on the solving of a mystery. Plots of mysteries often revolve around a crime. The hero must solve the mystery, overcoming unknown forces or enemies. Stories about detectives, police, private investigators, amateur sleuths, spies, thrillers, and courtroom dramas usually fall into this genre.

Fable A fable is a short story that states a moral. Fables often use talking animals or animated objects as the main characters. The interaction of the animals or animated objects reveals general truths about human nature.

Fairy Tale These tales are usually about elves, dragons, goblins, fairies, or magical beings and are often set in the distant past. Fairy tales usually begin with the phrase "Once upon a time . . ." and end with the words ". . . and they lived happily ever after." Charms, disguises, and talking animals may also appear in fairy tales.

Fantasy A fantasy may be any text or story removed from reality. Stories may be set in nonexistent worlds, such as an elf kingdom, on another planet, or in alternate versions of the known world. The characters may not be human (dragons, trolls, etc.) or may be humans who interact with non-human characters.

Folktale Stories that have been passed from one generation to the next by word of mouth rather than by written form are folktales. Folktales may include sayings, superstitions, social rituals, legends, or lore about the weather, animals, or plants.

Play Plays are specific pieces of drama, usually enacted on a stage by actors dressed in makeup and appropriate costumes.

Adventure Exciting events and actions feature in these stories. Character development, themes, or symbolism are not as important as the actions or events in an adventure story.

Humor Humor involves characters or events that promote laughter, pleasure, or humor in the reader.

Poetry This genre utilizes rhythmic patterns of language. The patterns include meter (high- and low-stressed syllables), syllabication (the number of syllables in each line), rhyme, alliteration, or a combination of these. Poems often use figurative language.

Genre Definitions *(cont.)*

Fiction and Poetry *(cont.)*

Myth
A myth explains a belief, practice, or natural phenomenon and usually involves gods, demons, or supernatural beings. A myth does not necessarily have a basis in fact or a natural explanation.

Legend
Legends are told as though the events were actual historical events. Legends may or may not be based on an elaborated version of a historical event. Legends are usually about human beings, although gods may intervene in some way throughout the story.

Nonfiction

Persuasive/Exposition
Written to persuade others to a particular point of view, expositions begin with a statement of the writer's position on an issue. This is followed by arguments with supporting details, such as evidence and examples. Rhetorical questions are included in expositions to encourage the reader to agree with the writer's point of view.

Explanation
These writings explain how or why something happens or has happened. They should include cause and effects, and a summarizing paragraph.

Reports
Reports are written documents describing the findings of an individual or group. They may take the form of a newspaper report, sports or police report, or a report about an animal, person, or object.

Biography
A biography is an account of a person's life written by another person. The biography may be about the life of a celebrity or a historical figure.

Autobiography
An autobiography is a piece of writing in which a writer uses his/her own life as the basis for a biography.

Journal
A journal is a continued series of texts written by a person about his/her life experiences and events. Journals may include descriptions of daily events as well as thoughts and emotions.

Review
A review is a concise summary or critical evaluation of a text, event, object, or phenomenon. A review may give a perspective, argument, or purpose. It offers critical assessment of content, effectiveness, noteworthy features, and often ends with a suggestion of audience appreciation.

Other **informational texts**, such as **timetables**, are excellent sources to teach and assess comprehension skills. Others may include **diagrams**, **graphs**, **advertisements**, **maps**, **plans**, **tables**, **charts**, **lists**, **posters**, and **programs**.

Genre: Fantasy

READING FOCUS

- Analyzes and extracts information from a fantasy narrative to answer literal, inferential, and applied questions
- Predicts the actions of characters based on background knowledge and information provided in the text
- Compares and makes connections within the text and between the text and himself/herself

ANSWER KEY

Literal (Page 11)

  1. True   2. False   3. True   4. False   5. False   6. False

Inferential (Page 11)

1. He had been to the surface often and had only seen an empty world of sky and waves.

2. through Sebastian and the other "swimmers"

3. "Swimmers" were the ones that were able to breathe underwater through gills, which allowed them to venture out from the dome to harvest food for the community.

Applied (Page 12)

1. a. from dry land

    b. The text mentions that Melissa has seen pictures of a similar mouse in old story books, most likely back when there was dry land.

2. The black bird came from dry land.

3. follow the black bird west in search of the dry land and establish a home on dry land

4. Answers will vary.

Applying Strategies (Page 13)

1–3. Answers will vary.

EXTENSIONS

- Brainstorm and list factors that may have contributed to such a major environmental disaster.
- Compile a list of characters from fantasy books and films. Identify any of their non-human characteristics and classify them as "good" or "evil."
- Discuss the effectiveness of leaving "what happens next" to the reader's imagination.

Name _____

Read the fantasy story and answer the questions on the following pages.

Sebastian looked up toward the surface of the water in amazement. It was like no creature he had ever seen before. Forgetting the constant task of finding more food to take back to the dome, he circled it cautiously. He breathed slowly through his gills—the legacy of being born a "swimmer." And just like his ancestors, he ventured out from the dome to harvest underwater vegetation—being the sea creature on which their community depended on.

After the land was inundated, his people had moved into a dome they had constructed in preparation for the inevitable disaster caused by the melting polar ice. He had visited the surface often—it was a bleak, empty world of sky and waves. The beautiful, dry world of the past he had learned about in old movies and books fascinated him. Unlike most of his friends, he believed that it could, after all these years, rise again from the oceans covering the Earth. He would love to venture farther afield in search of land, but there were only a few "swimmers," and the community depended on them.

On closer inspection, he found that the creature, about the size of a small whale, had the strangest skin and didn't acknowledge or respond to him. He pushed himself up above the surface but immediately dove back in confusion. The creature was carrying three beings who looked like people but with darker skin and lots of hair. As Sebastian's mind raced, he remembered hearing about how before the great flood, some people had constructed huge, floating, self-sufficient facilities on which whole communities had planned to live on.

The beings appeared very weak, and he realized that they were in need of water and food. There was no way that they could survive being taken down to the dome. He was curious to know more about them, so he decided to provide the immediate help they needed.

Michael, Melissa, and Brad certainly added interest and entertainment to Sebastian's life. He made daily visits with supplies and watched their rapid return to health. They were a constant source of amazement to Sebastian's community, especially to the other "swimmers," but the three would not stay for long. They were very anxious to resume their desperate search for land. Returning to their floating community, which was unable to survive for more than a few months, however was no longer an option.

A large black bird that had been circling the boat for some time landed on the stern and seemed to be staring at them with its enormous blue eyes. It was unlike any of the seabirds they occasionally saw diving for fish. The bird seemed to be holding something in its beak. It flew over and dropped something at Melissa's feet. A tiny creature lay very still, hardly breathing on the deck. Melissa picked it up by the tail, identifying it as a kind of mouse similar to some she had seen in old story books. They stared in wonder as the bird squawked at them and slowly, ever so slowly, started to fly toward the west.

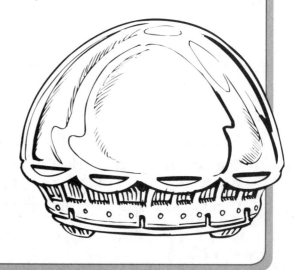

WATER WORLD

Literal Find the answers directly in the text.

Read each sentence. Decide if each statement is **True** or **False**.

1. Sebastian could breathe underwater. ☐ True ☐ False

2. Everyone who lived in the dome could breathe underwater. ☐ True ☐ False

3. People knew about the flood before it happened. ☐ True ☐ False

4. Sebastian was chosen to be a "swimmer." ☐ True ☐ False

5. Melissa, Michael, and Brad were floating on a whale. ☐ True ☐ False

6. Michael picked up the mouse. ☐ True ☐ False

Inferential Think about what the text says.

1. Why was Sebastian so surprised to meet Melissa, Michael, and Brad?

_____

_____

_____

2. How did most of the community living in the dome know about the visitors?

_____

_____

_____

3. Why did Sebastian's community depend on "swimmers"?

_____

_____

_____

WATER WORLD

Use what you know about the text and your own experience.

1. **a.** Where did the mouse most likely come from?

   _____

   _____

   b. Explain why you think this.

   _____

   _____

2. Why did the black bird look different from the seabirds?

   _____

   _____

3. What will Melissa, Michael, and Brad most likely do now?

   _____

   _____

   _____

   _____

   _____

4. Do you think Sebastian will stay in the dome? Explain why you think this.

   _____

   _____

   _____

   _____

   _____

   _____

WATER WORLD

Making Connections

Complete the following activities by linking your prior knowledge with new information from the text.

1. If you had to live for generations on a huge floating structure, like Melissa, Michael, and Brad's ancestors did, what would be some of the major difficulties you would need to overcome? How could they be managed?

Hurdles	Possible Solutions

2. What were be some of the difficulties Sebastian's ancestors may have had to overcome living in the dome?

Hurdles	Possible Solutions

3. Which of the two situations for surviving a flood do you prefer?

Comparing

_____

Explain why you prefer this. _____

_____

_____

Unit 2
The Rocket Builder

Genre: Fictitious Autobiography

Teacher Information

READING FOCUS

- Analyzes and extracts information from an autobiography to answer literal, inferential, and applied questions
- Makes predictions about the responses of characters in a text
- Makes comparisons between the text and himself/herself

ANSWER KEY

Literal (Page 16)

1. True   2. False   3. False   4. True   5. True   6. False

Inferential (Page 16)

1. Jake didn't have a television at home.

2. Answers will vary. Possible answer(s): rockets were a very new technology at that time, and only a few books were published about rockets; all the other books may have been checked out due to the popularity of the *Sputnik* launch.

3. A flat area would allow the rocket to be positioned upright and more likely fly straight up instead of sideways.

4. a. Answers will vary. Possible answer(s): excited, eager, motivated, ambitious, at times frustrated or doubtful.

   b. Answers will vary. Possible answer(s): nervous, excited, accomplished, hopeful.

Applied (Page 17)

1–3. Answers will vary.

Applying Strategies (Page 18)

1–3. Answers will vary.

EXTENSIONS

- Students can use a search engine to find out about the life of a person who interests them. Students write a profile about the person they have researched.
- Watch the movie *October Sky*, and make comparisons between the characters Homer Hickam and Jake Gilligan.

Name _____

Read the chapter from this fictitious autobiography and answer the questions on the following pages.

An excerpt from the fictitious autobiography of NASA scientist Jake Gilligan.

Chapter Three

October 1957

I had been waiting outside of Finley's Electronics for over an hour—determined to get a good position. With my nose pressed against the glass, I watched the launch of *Sputnik* on seven different televisions. She looked so beautiful when all of the engines were fired up, launching her into the sky and Earth's orbit.

I was so excited after the launch that I rode straight over and met up with Dave and Gerry. We rode to the Fairfield Library and borrowed the only two books we could find about rockets. We passed them around the table, looking at the photographs and diagrams in amazement.

Before I had even realized what I was saying, I had announced to the gang that we were going to build a rocket. Of course, the boys were skeptical, saying that our fathers would think it was a waste of time, and the kids at school would tease us. The boys were right, but as I said to them, none of us was ever going to get noticed in this town by being big football stars, so why not try and build a rocket instead?

We decided that Gerry's basement would be the perfect location to build a rocket, so we took the books down there. Luckily, Gerry's dad was out playing a round of golf, so we didn't have to explain our plans. We could all imagine what our fathers would say . . .

"You are just wasting your time building rockets. Do you actually think you will leave Fairfield and become a rocket scientist? I don't think so. Go outside and play football instead."

That week, we spoke to Miss Warner, the science teacher, and told her about our project. She was very excited and gave us a leaflet about the state science competition that was being held in December. We now had a deadline! Whenever we could get away, we would meet in Gerry's basement and discuss and design our rocket. We started to collect materials and tools, and soon after, we were sawing or sanding away. I would also ride over to my Uncle Stan's mechanic shop whenever we needed parts welded together.

By the third of December we were finished! We walked up to the hills behind the town, looking for a launch site and found a flat area that was perfect. We also discovered a piece of discarded steel that we could use for protection in case our rocket decided to fly sideways instead of up!

Gerry, Dave, and I chose a long fuse for our first rocket. I lit it and we ran behind the steel, peering out over the top.

Our first launch. We counted down together . . .

"10, 9, 8, 7, 6, 5, 4, 3, 2, 1 . . . Blast off!"

THE ROCKET BUILDER

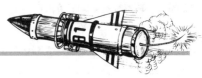

| **Literal** | Find the answers directly in the text. |

Read each sentence. Decide if each statement is **True** or **False**.

1. According to the text, Jake Gilligan became a rocket scientist at NASA. ☐ True ☐ False

2. *Sputnik* was launched into Earth's orbit in October 1967. ☐ True ☐ False

3. The Fairfield Library had many books about building rockets. ☐ True ☐ False

4. The boys wanted to be noticed, so they built a rocket. ☐ True ☐ False

5. Jake believed his dad would tell him to play football instead of building rockets. ☐ True ☐ False

6. *Miss Warner* was the boys' English teacher. ☐ True ☐ False

| **Inferential** | Think about what the text says. |

1. In 1957, Jake Gilligan watched the launch of *Sputnik* on television through a store window. What is the most likely reason he didn't watch it at home?

   _____

2. Why do you think the Fairfield Library only had two books about rockets?

   _____

3. Why was a flat area ideal for launching the rocket?

   _____

4. List words or phrases to describe how you think the boys were feeling when:

   a. they were in Gerry's basement, building their rocket.

   _____

   _____

   b. they were crouched behind the steel as the fuse burnt down to ignite their rocket.

   _____

   _____

THE ROCKET BUILDER

Applied Use what you know about the text and your own experience.

1. Even though the boys knew their fathers would be unhappy about them wasting their time building a rocket, they went ahead and built one. Why do you think this is?

   _____

   _____

   _____

   _____

2. What do you think the kids at school thought about Dave, Gerry, and Jake after they heard about the rocket the boys had built?

   _____

   _____

   _____

3. Write about a time when you were so excited about doing something that you didn't care what others would think of you.

   _____

   _____

   _____

   _____

   _____

   _____

   _____

   _____

   _____

THE ROCKET BUILDER

Predicting

Use the text on page 15 to complete the following activity. The launch was a success! The boys ran back to town and told everyone who would listen about their rocket.

1. Predict what each person would say about the boys and their rocket.

Miss Warner:

_____

_____

Jake's father:

_____

_____

Journalist for the *Fairfield Times* newspaper:

_____

_____

Judge at the state science competition:

_____

_____

2. **a.** The text shows just one chapter of Jake Gilligan's autobiography. With a partner, discuss what you think the other chapters in the autobiography would be about. Write three questions that you would like answered about Jake Gilligan's life. List them below.

- _____
- _____
- _____

b. Choose one question above. Discuss with a partner what you think the answer might be. Write the answer you agreed upon below.

_____

_____

3. It is the year 2050, and you are writing your own autobiography. How will your life story be similar to or different from Jake Gilligan's autobiography? Make notes below.

Comparing

Similar	Different

Genre: Folktale

READING FOCUS

- Analyzes and extracts information from a folktale to answer literal, inferential, and applied questions
- Predicts the conversation of two characters based on information provided in the text
- Scans text to identify main messages
- Compares and makes connections between the text and own life to create a role-play

ANSWER KEY

Literal (Page 21)

1. a. happy; mud hut   b. minutes   c. need anything from him

   d. a new washtub   e. sympathy

2. a. a new washtub   b. a new house   c. become queen

   d. find the old mud hut and his wife standing next to the broken washtub

Inferential (Page 21)

1. The wife was full of anger, demanding, greedy, and self-seeking. The fisherman was kind-hearted, selfless, and humble.

2. - brilliant blue and calm

   - small waves

   - swirling currents and larger waves

   - nearly black, and wild and raging

Applied (Page 22)

1–2. Answers will vary.

3. greed leads to grief

Applying Strategies (Page 23)

1–2. Answers will vary.

EXTENSIONS

- Many websites dedicated to folktales can be found on the Internet. Some suggested websites include the following:
  - *www.americanfolklore.net*
  - *www.kidsgen.com/stories/folk_tales/*
  - *www.pitara.com/talespin/folktales.asp*
- Students can perform their role-plays to a younger class. After the role-play, ask the students whether they know what the message of the play was.

Name _____

Read the folktale and answer the questions on the following pages.

A very poor but happy couple lived in a mud hut at the edge of the sea. The husband was a fisherman. Each day, he would venture down to the ocean and fish so that he and his wife would have something to eat that night. His wife would spin cloth so that they would have clothes to wear.

One day, just like every other day, the fisherman walked down to the brilliant blue, calm sea and began to fish. What luck! Within minutes, there was a tug at the end of his line. The fisherman reeled the fish in and collected it in his net. To his surprise, the fish was a dazzling golden color.

"Please, kind fisherman, spare me my life," the golden fish pleaded. "If you do, in return I will grant you any wish you desire."

The kind-hearted fisherman was surprised, as he had never heard a fish speak before. He put the little fish back into the water and said, "Thank you, but I do not need anything from you."

That night, during their evening meal, the fisherman told his wife about the golden fish. Her face turned red with anger. She stood and screamed furiously at her husband.

"How could you have not made a wish when I have to wash our clothes in a broken washtub each day? You are a fool!"

The next morning, the fisherman returned to the sea, which had lost its brilliant blue color, and small waves now crashed against the shore. The fisherman called out to the golden fish who swam up to the fisherman.

Humbly, the fisherman bowed and asked the fish, "My wife is very angry with me for not wishing for a new washtub." The golden fish comforted the man and said he would grant the wish.

The fisherman returned home, happily anticipating his wife's delight, but alas, although his wife stood next to her new washtub, she cursed him angrily.

"You are a silly fool! Why did you not wish a new house for us? Go back tomorrow, and ask the fish for a house!"

The fisherman arrived at the sea the following day. Swirling currents pulled at the water and larger waves crashed into the shore. The fisherman knelt down on the sand and called for the fish. He apologized, explaining that his wife was angered that he had not wished for a new house.

The golden fish sympathized with the fisherman and granted him his wish. That night, the fisherman returned home to his wife, who was standing, hands on hips, inside their beautiful new cottage. She was enraged!

"It's not enough!" she cried. "Go back tomorrow. I wish to be queen!"

When the fisherman returned to the sea the next day, he saw it was nearly black in color, and the water was wild and raging. Feeling disheartened, he once again called to the fish and told him of his wife's request. The fish turned and swam away from the fisherman.

The fisherman returned home, where he found a mud hut and his wife sitting next to a broken washtub.

THE GOLDEN FISH

Literal   Find the answers directly in the text.

1. Locate word(s) in the text to complete each sentence.

   a. In the beginning, the poor couple was _____, living in a

   _____ at the edge of the sea.

   b. The fisherman caught the golden fish within _____ of casting.

   c. The kind-hearted fisherman initially told the golden fish that he did not _____

   _____.

   d. The wife first demanded _____.

   e. The golden fish felt _____ for the fisherman.

2. Complete the chain of events in the folktale "The Golden Fish."

   Fisherman catches the golden fish.

   a. Wife asks for _____.

   b. Wife asks for _____.

   c. Wife asks to _____.

   d. Fisherman returns home to _____

   _____.

Inferential   Think about what the text says.

1. How was the wife different from the fisherman?

   _____

   _____

2. Make notes to show how the sea changed throughout the story.

   • _____   • _____

   • _____   • _____

THE GOLDEN FISH

Applied   Use what you know about the text and your own experience.

1. What do you think the changes in the appearance of the sea mean in the story?

   _____

   _____

   _____

   _____

2. If you were fishing and caught the golden fish, what would you wish for?

   _____

   _____

   _____

   _____

3. What is the main message or lesson from the story?

   _____

   _____

   _____

   _____

   _____

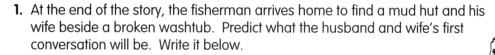

Applying Strategies

THE GOLDEN FISH

Predicting

1. At the end of the story, the fisherman arrives home to find a mud hut and his wife beside a broken washtub. Predict what the husband and wife's first conversation will be. Write it below.

Husband	Wife

2. **a.** Create a plan for a new play that takes place in the present time and has a similar message to "The Golden Fish."

Comparing

Title: "The Golden Fish"	**Title:**
Setting: On the edge of the sea.	**Setting:**
Characters: • The humble fisherman • The greedy wife • The golden fish	**Characters:** • _____ • _____ • _____
Plot: Fisherman catches a golden fish that can grant wishes. Greedy wife asks for more and more wishes until she goes too far, and the golden fish erases all the granted wishes.	**Plot:**

b. Practice and present your short play to a small group or the class.

Genre: Fairy Tale

READING FOCUS

- Analyzes and extracts information from a fairy tale to answer literal, inferential, and applied questions
- Predicts information about a character and considers his/her own choices if placed in a similar situation
- Makes connections between a text and a well-known fairy tale to synthesize the conventions of the fairy-tale genre

ANSWER KEY

Literal (Page 26)

1. Princess Bella earned her nickname of "Brooding Bella" because she rarely smiled.

2. The princess stopped and listened to the conversation in the kitchen because she thought there may be an opportunity for her to leave the castle.

3. The princess was imagining that she was flying away from the castle forever.

4. The princess blushed and stormed away. She then decided to catch the frogs herself using the hood of her cloak.

5. Princess Bella did get what she had wished for, which was to travel the land having many adventures.

Inferential (Page 26)

1. Answers will vary. Possible answer(s): The cook was hesitant to let the princess leave the castle because the King may get upset about his daughter helping the staff.

2. Answers will vary.

3. Answers will vary. Possible answer(s): Princess Bella may have found it amusing that her first kiss came from a frog.

4. Answers will vary. Possible answer(s): adventurous, determined, clever.

Applied (Page 27)

1–3. Answers will vary.

Applying Strategies (Page 28)

1–3. Answers will vary.

EXTENSIONS

- Read other fairy tales and fractured fairy tales, such as the following titles:
  - *Snow White in New York* by Fiona French
  - *Princess Smartypants* by Babette Cole
  - *The Paper Bag Princess* by Robert Munsch
  - *Revolting Rhymes* by Roald Dahl
  - *Legally Correct Fairy Tales* by David Fisher

Name _____

Read the fairy tale and answer the questions on the following pages.

Once upon a time, in a faraway land, lived a beautiful but unhappy princess. Princess Bella lived in an enormous castle with her mother and father. She had an extravagant bedroom and maids to clean it for her. She could request any meal she liked and the cooks would prepare it, and she could attend the grandest parties in the land. Even though Princess Bella had all her needs and comforts met, she was known in the land as "Brooding Bella" because she rarely smiled.

"I wish I had the freedom to leave the castle and have many adventures traveling across all the land," she would weep quietly each night into her pillow.

One day, the princess was in the castle walking past the kitchen when she heard the head cook announce that the King was having noblemen from France to dinner.

"The only thing is," the cook discussed with his staff, "I haven't any frogs to make garlic frog legs!"

Princess Bella, hearing an opportunity for her to leave the castle, entered the kitchen.

"I shall take Bolt, my fastest stallion, and ride to the markets to purchase some frogs for this evening's supper," she said with authority.

The cook was most pleased but felt that the princess should inform her father of her journey. The princess, thinking quickly, replied, "Father would be very angry if we bothered him when he is preparing for his meeting with the French Ambassador."

The cook hesitantly agreed, and soon after, Princess Bella was galloping across the meadows toward the village. As the wind caught her long auburn hair, she imagined that she was flying away from the castle forever.

Arriving at the markets, the princess put on her long, dark cloak and covered her head in its hood—she was not in the mood for bowing commoners today. She walked briskly toward the stall with skinned animals hanging from large hooks and chickens waiting to be plucked.

"Two dozen frog legs," she ordered from the man behind the stall.

The butcher leaned toward her, the stench of raw flesh entering the princess's nose, making her sneeze. "Two dozen, eh?" he said, greedily rubbing his hands together. "You must have a hefty purse for that order."

The princess, realizing she hadn't brought any money with her, blushed and stormed away—angry with her own absent-mindedness. Never one to give up, Princess Bella walked to a nearby stream. Removing her cloak, she decided that she would catch some frogs in its hood. The princess's auburn hair fell around her face, and the sun's rays gleamed on her exquisite gown.

Hearing a croaking sound, the princess knelt down on the bank and parted the leaves of a nearby bush. Just as she moved closer to the bush, a frog made a giant leap toward the princess's face. The princess was startled by the frog that had just left a slimy, wet patch on her cheek. She wiped it away and surprisingly began to smile.

"Why, little frog," Princess Bella said in a light-hearted tone (realizing she had just experienced her very first kiss). "I do believe you just kissed me."

The frog bounced over to a lily pad and stared back at the princess.

"I did, (ribbit)," said the frog. "I am Beau, the frog prince, (ribbit). I have been waiting for seven (ribbit) years for a beautiful princess to come to the (ribbit) stream so I could kiss her."

As soon as the frog prince stopped speaking, the princess started to feel strange. Her body began to tingle, and a magical silver shine spread its way across her body. Within a few seconds, the princess had transformed into a frog.

The two frogs hopped away from the village along the banks of the stream. Together they traveled across all the land, having many adventures and feeling very free. The frog prince and his princess lived happily ever after.

PRINCESS BELLA AND THE FROG PRINCE

Literal   Find the answers directly in the text.

1. How did Princess Bella earn her nickname?

   _____

2. What made the princess stop and listen to the head cook's conversation with his staff?

   _____

3. What was the princess imagining as she rode toward the markets?

   _____

   _____

4. Describe how the princess reacted when she couldn't buy the frog legs.

   _____

   _____

5. Princess Bella lived happily ever after. Did she get what she had wished for?

   _____

   _____

Inferential   Think about what the text says.

1. Why was the cook hesitant to let the princess leave the castle?

   _____

2. Do you think the princess had been to the markets before? Why do you think this?

   _____

   _____

3. Why do you think the princess smiled after the frog leaped at her from behind the bush?

   _____

4. Describe some of the qualities Princess Bella possessed.

   _____

   _____

PRINCESS BELLA AND THE FROG PRINCE

Applied   Use what you know about the text and your own experience.

1. If you were in Princess Bella's situation, living with your family in a castle, would you be unhappy? Explain.

_____

_____

_____

_____

_____

2. If you could travel across any land having many adventures, where would you go, and who would you go with?

_____

_____

_____

_____

_____

_____

3. Imagine you were Princess Bella. You had a choice of either staying human but being stuck in the castle, or turning into a frog and be free to have many adventures. Which would you choose and why?

_____

_____

_____

_____

_____

_____

PRINCESS BELLA AND THE FROG PRINCE

Use the fairy tale on page 25 to complete the following activities and make comparisons.

1. While Princess Bella lived in the castle, she had the comforts of home and many luxuries. Add details to describe her life in the castle. What would you choose if you could live like a princess or a prince? Complete the table for both Princess Bella and yourself.

	Princess Bella	Your Own Choice
Have an enormous, extravagant bedroom. What was it like?		
Request any meal and the cooks will make it. What type of meals?		
Attend the grandest parties in the land. What type of parties?		

2. Summarize the main components of the fairy tale from page 25 in the table below. Choose another fairy tale that you are the most familiar with to complete the table.

Fairy Tale 1
Title: Princess Bella and the Frog Prince
Main Characters:
Plot:
Ending: ☐ Happy ☐ Sad

Fairy Tale 2
Title:
Main Characters:
Plot:
Ending: ☐ Happy ☐ Sad

3. Compare your summaries above. Write three attributes a fairy tale should include. Discuss your ideas with a partner.

   • _____

   • _____

   • _____

Unit 5
Petrified Wood

Genre: Suspense

Teacher Information

READING FOCUS

- Analyzes and extracts information from a suspense narrative to answer literal, inferential, and applied questions
- Makes connections between the text and his/her own experiences
- Predicts how a character will react to a specific object when the setting changes from night to day

ANSWER KEY

Literal (Page 31)

1. his dad is on a business trip
2. pay for Joey's hockey club membership and buy him the new stick he wanted.
3. he is too scared of the tree outside his window.

Inferential (Page 31)

1. Joey wasn't old enough to stay home alone.
2. The text mentioned that Joey had puffy, dark circles underneath his eyes the last time his dad picked him up. This was most likely from a lack of sleep.
3. Answers will vary. Possible answer(s): Joey may have been embarrassed and felt that he was being childish.
4. Answers will vary.

Applied (Page 32)

1–4. Answers will vary.

Applying Strategies (Page 33)

1–2. Answers will vary.

EXTENSIONS

- Students can compile lists of authors of the suspense genre and titles, such as the *Goosebumps* series by R.L. Stein.
- Students can draw or paint a picture of the tree described in the story, and write a poem describing its spooky features.

Name _____

Read the suspense story and answer the questions on the following pages.

Joey is back in the uncomfortable bed with the lumpy pillow and the gray "army blanket" that makes him itch. His whole body is turned toward the wall. The spare room at his Aunt Jean's house is on the first floor, and right outside is a very large tree that fills the window, blocking all else from view. The tree moves with the wind—its branches rubbing up against the window—scraping and scratching at the glass.

Joey's dad had promised him the time before this that it would be his last business trip for a while. But, here Joey is again, staying overnight at his aunt's. Surely Joey's dad had noticed the puffy, dark circles underneath his eyes when he picked him up from Jean's the last time? But he hadn't asked why Joey had looked so tired. He just talked about how well the business trip went and told Joey that he would now be able to pay for his hockey club membership and buy Joey the new stick he wanted.

Joey, tense with fear and eyes glued shut, listens to the scraping against the glass. If he could move his hands from underneath the sheets, he would cover his ears, but his limbs seem paralyzed in place. It is as though the tree is moving side to side, trying to get a better look in the window, and at Joey.

Joey shudders and curls up into a tight ball. He repeats over and over in his head—"It's just a tree. It's just a tree."

When Joey's body starts to ache from being in one position for so long and his lungs hurt from holding his breath, he becomes angry with himself for being so childish and summons up the courage to turn his head and stare directly at the tree. Its thick trunk has round holes where branches once were. They look like black eyes watching him in his bed. The branches have swollen knots that look like elbows, and the tips of the branches are bare of leaves. Joey imagines they are stick-thin fingers with sharp nails. He is certain that a strong gust of wind will allow them to pierce the thin glass of the bedroom window.

A screeching sound tears through the night. "Bats! They must be in the tree!" Joey thinks.

He quickly turns over and lies flat on his stomach. The hairs on the back of his neck stand on end, and his face is full of pillow—the cotton entering his nose with every quick breath he takes. His arms are tight by his sides now (just in case there's anything underneath the bed!).

Joey stays frozen like this for the longest time, wishing over and over that he could just fall asleep.

Meanwhile, Aunt Jean's cat climbs up her favorite tree and onto one of the branches. The cat, purring and licking her paws, stares in the window. Her cat mouth is turned upward, almost as if she is smiling at the frightened little boy lying like a piece of petrified wood in his bed.

PETRIFIED WOOD

Literal	Find the answers directly in the text.

Complete the following sentences.

1. Joey is staying at his aunt's house because _____

   _____ .

2. Joey's dad was excited because he could afford to _____

   _____ .

3. Joey can't get to sleep because _____

   _____ .

Inferential	Think about what the text says.

1. Why do you think Joey couldn't stay at home when his dad went away on the trip?

   _____

2. What evidence from the text shows that Joey had a similar experience the last time he slept at his aunt's house?

   _____

3. Why do you think Joey didn't tell his dad about being frightened of the tree?

   _____

4. Do you think the tree would look as scary during the day? Explain your answer.

   _____

   _____

   _____

PETRIFIED WOOD

Applied Use what you know about the text and your own experience.

1. How old do you think Joey is? Explain your answer.

_____

_____

_____

2. In the story, Joey becomes angry with himself for being such a baby. Who do you think might have called him a "baby" in the past?

_____

_____

_____

3. Why do you think Joey was so scared of the tree? Explain your ideas.

_____

_____

_____

_____

4. Write about a time when your imagination got the best of you.

_____

_____

_____

_____

_____

_____

PETRIFIED WOOD

Use the text on page 30 to complete the following activities. When you read a story, your memories of your own experiences, people that you know, and the things you have read about or have seen in movies can be triggered. This is called "making connections" with the text.

1. What connections did you make when you read "Petrified Wood"? Complete the sentences below.

a. The story reminds me of a time when _____

_____

_____.

b. The character of Joey reminds me of _____ because

_____

_____.

2. Imagine that it is the next morning. Joey eats his breakfast and goes outside to discover that it is a glorious and bright, sunny day. He looks up at the tree, shielding his eyes from the sun.

How do you think Joey's perception of the tree may have changed from the night before? Add words and phrases to describe how Joey might see the tree during the day.

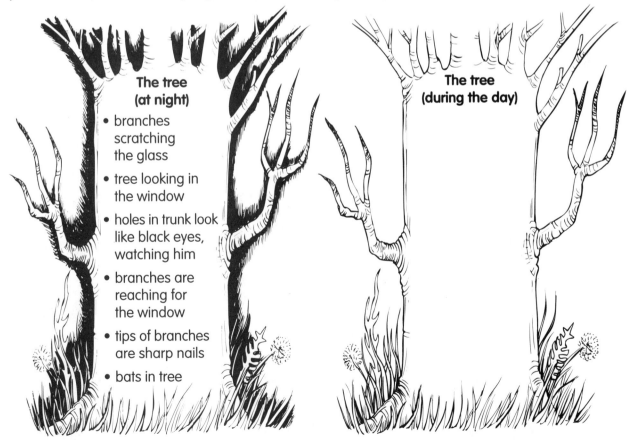

The tree (at night)
- branches scratching the glass
- tree looking in the window
- holes in trunk look like black eyes, watching him
- branches are reaching for the window
- tips of branches are sharp nails
- bats in tree

The tree (during the day)

Genre: Explanation

READING FOCUS

- Analyzes and extracts information from an explanation to answer literal, inferential, and applied questions
- Makes connections between his/her own ideas and new information presented in a text to plan a speech
- Determines the importance of information contained in a text

---

ANSWER KEY

Literal (Page 36)

1. 1812   Punctured his eye with a sharp tool

     1819   Went to the Royal Institution for Blind Youth

     1821   His school was visited by a French army captain

     1824   Invented braille

2. a. False   b. True   c. False   d. False

Inferential (Page 36)

1. Answers will vary. Possible answer(s): It may have taken too long to feel every single letter and form a word.

2. Answers will vary. Possible answer(s): intelligent—able to learn just by listening to his teacher and went to the Royal Institution for Blind Youth at the age of 10; innovative—he felt that the way blind people read could be improved upon, and he invented the braille system; determined—it took him three years to develop the braille system.

Applied (Page 37)

1–2. Answers will vary.

Applying Strategies (Page 38)

1. Answers will vary. Possible answer(s): Braille is a way to read independently without the use of technology; it starts with the basics of reading letters; many books and other products are available that use braille.

2. Answers will vary. Possible answer(s): Just like learning to write with pencil and paper, braille is the introduction to writing for blind or visually impaired people.

3. Answers will vary.

EXTENSIONS

- Students can conduct an online search to learn more about the braille system.
- Students can write their name using the six-dot braille system.

BRAILLE

Name _____

Read the explanation and answer the questions on the following pages.

Braille is a type of code used by people who are blind or visually impaired to read and write. It uses raised dots that are felt with the fingers.

Braille was invented by a 15-year-old French boy. His name was Louis Braille. Louis was born in France in 1809. When he was three years old, he was playing in his father's shoemaking workshop and punctured his eye with a sharp tool. His eye became infected, and the infection soon spread to the other eye, leaving him completely blind.

Louis went to school with sighted children where he learned by listening to his teachers. When he was 10 years old, Louis went to the Royal Institution for Blind Youth in Paris. Here, he learned to read by feeling raised letters on a page. The letters had been made by pressing copper wire into the paper. Although Louis was thrilled to read, he felt that the method could be improved upon—it was cumbersome and provided no way for blind people to write.

In 1821, the school was visited by a French army captain. He had invented a code for soldiers to use that could be read on battlefields at night without needing light. The code used raised dots to represent sounds. Louis experimented with this concept, and in 1824, he developed a simplified version of the code that represented normal spelling—the braille system.

The basis of the braille system is called a "cell." A cell is made up of six dots and looks like this:

Each letter of the alphabet is made up of one or more of these dots. For example,
p = and r =

If you were to learn braille, you would begin by learning the letters and putting them together to form words. Once you were an expert at this, you would learn a kind of braille shorthand, where dots represent words. This means that you could read more quickly and less paper would be used. You could also learn to read braille cells that represent numbers, punctuation marks, and even musical notes.

The simplest way to write braille is using a slate and a stylus. A sheet of paper is placed into the slate, and the stylus is used to push dots into the paper. Braille can also be written with braille writers (like typewriters) or electronic machines called "braillers." A brailler can be plugged into a computer where the braille can be read by a voice synthesizer or printed out as normal typescript.

Today, braille has been adapted to almost every language in the world and is accepted as the standard form of reading and writing for blind or visually impaired people. There are braille books, musical scores, playing cards, watches, board games, and many other materials.

BRAILLE

| **Literal** | Find the answers directly in the text. |

1. Write a fact for each date in Louis Braille's life.

   1812 _____

   1819 _____

   1821 _____

   1824 _____

2. Read each sentence. Decide if each statement is **True** or **False**.

   a. Louis Braille punctured both his eyes with a sharp tool. ☐ True ☐ False

   b. You can do math problems using braille. ☐ True ☐ False

   c. English is the only language that can be written in braille. ☐ True ☐ False

   d. Each letter in braille contains at least five dots. ☐ True ☐ False

| **Inferential** | Think about what the text says. |

1. Why do you think the way Louis Braille first learned to read is described as "cumbersome"?

   _____

   _____

2. List three words or phrases to describe Louis Braille, and include evidence from the text.

   • _____

   _____

   • _____

   _____

   • _____

   _____

BRAILLE

| **Applied** | Use what you know about the text and your own experience. |

1. Write three questions you would like to ask Louis Braille about his life or his invention.

   a. _____

   _____

   _____

   b. _____

   _____

   _____

   c. _____

   _____

   _____

2. Do you think the braille system should have also been named after the French army captain? Give reasons to support your opinion.

   _____

   _____

   _____

   _____

   _____

   _____

   _____

   _____

   _____

   _____

BRAILLE

Use the text on page 35 to help you complete this activity. Imagine you work for an international group that promotes the use of braille. You attend a conference about educating blind or visually impaired children. One speaker says the following:

> Blind or visually impaired children do not need to learn braille in today's world. It is old-fashioned. Teachers should be concentrating on modern technology instead; for example, teaching the children to listen to stories and record their own text in digital audio file format. Children can touch type on a computer keyboard and can then listen to the computer read their writing back to them.

The conference organizers have asked you to respond to this speech. They want you to explain why braille should still be taught to blind or visually impaired children. Write some notes for your speech in the space below.

1. Write some reasons why you think children should learn to *read* in braille.

    _____

    _____

    _____

2. Write some reasons why you think children should learn to *write* in braille.

    _____

    _____

    _____

3. What do you think of what the speaker said? Write what you agreed or disagreed with, and why.

    _____

    _____

    _____

    _____

    _____

    _____

Unit 7
Lone Survivor!

Genre: Journal

Teacher Information

READING FOCUS

- Analyzes and extracts information from a journal to answer literal, inferential, and applied questions
- Scans text to identify relevant events
- Makes connections between text and a character's emotions
- Compares similarities and differences between interpretations of text
- Predicts the next entry in a journal

ANSWER KEY

Literal (page 41)

1. True—". . . and once again we dig the dogs and sledges out of the snow after three long days of sheltering from yet another blizzard."
2. True—". . . fashion a tent out of a spare tent cover and drape it over skis to provide some shelter . . ."
3. False—"With what little strength I can gather, I haul Mertz by sledge to within 100 miles of base camp."

Inferential (page 41)

1. He most likely sawed the sledge in half to make it lighter to drag.
2. a. acute, severe (4)   b. writhes (4)   c. laboriously (1)   d. inevitable (2)
   e. whimpering (1)   f. presence (5)
3. - fashioned a tent out of spare tent cover and draped it over skis to provide some shelter
   - forced to feed the dogs worn-out fur boots, mitts, and rawhide straps
   - began sacrificing the dogs one by one to feed the other dogs and themselves

Applied (page 42)

1. a. 160 kilometers   b. 224 kilometers   c. 504 kilometers   d. 45 meters
2. Answers will vary.

Applying Strategies (Page 43)

1. Answers will vary. Possible answers:

Emotion	Incident	Emotion	Incident
Panic	". . . Mertz suddenly cries out in horror."	Despair	"It would be easier to let go and not get out . . ."
Hope	". . . I feel the presence of a spirit helping me . . ."	Pain	". . . my toes, fingers, and skin turning black with frostbite . . ."
Loneliness	"I am left alone to continue the journey . . ."		Answers will vary.

2–3. Answers will vary.

EXTENSIONS

- Students can use the Internet or locate nonfiction books in the library to discover more about Sir Douglas Mawson's expeditions to the Antarctic and his life in general.
- Other famous polar explorers include Roald Amundsen, Robert Scott, Robert E. Peary, Richard Byrd, Sir Ernest Henry Shackleton, and Sir James Clark Ross.

LONE SURVIVOR!

Name _____

Read the journal and answer the questions on the following pages.

Sir Douglas Mawson is one of several explorers who boldly led expeditions to investigate the harsh, frozen continent of Antarctica. In November 1912, Mawson and two other men, Xavier Mertz and Belgrave Ninnis, left base camp to map the continent to the east. It was to be a fateful journey, with Mawson being the lone survivor of a terrible ordeal. The journal extracts below are based on his experiences.

December 9–14, 1912

. . . and once again we dig the dogs and sledges out of the snow after three long days of sheltering from yet another blizzard. We continue to trek laboriously east, always on the lookout for deep crevasses hidden by thick snow. Mertz, who has gone ahead on skis, locates a snow-covered crevasse. Just as I make it safely across with my sledge, Mertz suddenly cries out in horror. The terrible feeling of dread fills my stomach. I turn around and realize Ninnis, his sledge, and six dogs have fallen into the crevasse. We stare into the gaping abyss and can only see one dog, whimpering in pain on a ledge some 150 feet below.

For hours, we call out to Ninnis, unable to accept his inevitable death. We cling to each other for comfort. Finally, Mertz and I take stock of supplies. Ninnis had the most important supplies on his sledge, along with the strongest dogs. This realization fills us with alarm. We wonder how we will survive the 315 miles back to base camp with only 10 days' rations and none for the remaining dogs . . .

December 15–30, 1912

. . . fashion a tent out of a spare tent cover and drape it over skis to provide some shelter . . . are forced to feed the dogs worn-out fur boots, mitts, and rawhide straps . . . focus on our goal of making it back to base camp, with hunger and bone-chilling cold trying to crush our spirit . . . begin to sacrifice the dogs one by one to feed the others and ourselves . . .

January 1–8, 1913

. . . still some 140 miles to go, and poor Mertz is extremely weak and has acute stomach pains of which I am suffering from less intensely. Both of us have severe frostbite. With what little strength I can gather, I haul Mertz by sledge to within 100 miles of base camp. He becomes delirious . . . put him in his sleeping bag and hold him down while he raves on and writhes in agony . . . finally he quiets down and dies peacefully in the morning . . . I am left alone to continue the journey . . . I lie in my bag with my spirits low and wonder how I can survive with little food and my toes, fingers, and skin turning black with frostbite . . .

January 9–February 8, 1913

. . . despite my suffering I manage to continue . . . I feel the presence of a spirit helping me, especially when I find myself dangling in a crevasse by my harness. It would be easier to let go and not get out . . . I saw my sledge in half and keep dragging my crippled body onward . . . finally, a welcome vision greets me. I have stumbled into base camp and stare into six disbelieving pairs of eyes—my colleagues who have stayed behind to continue the search . . .

Name _____

Activities

LONE SURVIVOR!

Literal   Find the answers directly in the text.

Read each sentence. Decide if each statement is **True** or **False**, and write a phrase or sentence from the text to prove your answer.

1. The three explorers had experienced several blizzards.   ☐ True ☐ False

_____

2. Mawson and Mertz were left without a tent after Ninnis's fall.   ☐ True ☐ False

_____

3. The dogs help Mawson to haul the sledge carrying Mertz.   ☐ True ☐ False

_____

Inferential   Think about what the text says.

1. What is the most likely reason Mawson sawed his sledge in half? _____

_____

2. Write a synonym from the text for each word below, and list the number of the journal paragraph it is found in the brackets. Use a dictionary, if needed.

a. extreme   _____ (____)   **b.** tosses   _____ (____)

c. arduously   _____ (____)   **d.** certain   _____ (____)

e. moaning   _____ (____)   **f.** company   _____ (____)

3. Mawson and Mertz were forced to make do when their necessary supplies fell into the crevasse. Scan the December 15–30 entry to describe three examples.

- _____

_____

- _____

_____

- _____

_____

©Teacher Created Resources   *41*   *#8249 Comprehending Text*

LONE SURVIVOR!

Applied   Use what you know about the text and your own experience.

1. Convert these distances in the journal from miles and feet to the nearest kilometer or meter. (1 mile = 1.6 kilometers, 1 foot = 0.3 meters)

   a. 100 miles = _____ kilometers

   b. 140 miles = _____ kilometers

   c. 315 miles = _____ kilometers

   d. 150 feet = _____ meters

2. Describe how you think Mawson could have escaped from the crevasse he fell into.

   _____

   _____

   _____

   _____

   _____

   _____

   _____

   _____

   _____

   _____

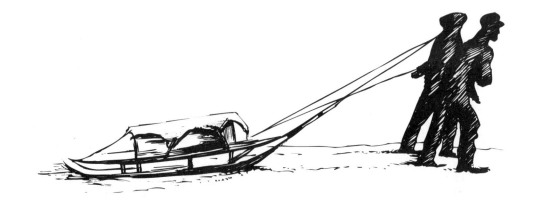

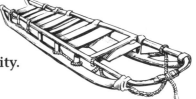

LONE SURVIVOR!

Scan the text on page 40 to help
you complete the following activity.

1. **a.** With a partner, scan the text to find and describe an incident that caused Mawson to experience
    each emotion listed below. Add an emotion of your own choice in the blank box.

    b. Compare your answers with other pairs of students in your class.

Emotion	Incident	Emotion	Incident
Panic		Despair	
Hope		Pain	
Loneliness			

2. Add more words and phrases to the list below to describe qualities Mawson possessed that helped him
    to survive. Discuss and compare with others in your class and list any more you think would be relevant.

    brave, thoughtful, _____

    _____

3. Imagine you are Mawson and have just stumbled into base camp, where your colleagues are staring
    in disbelief. Write your next journal entry.

    February 8, 1913 — _____

    _____

    _____

    _____

Genre: Biography

READING FOCUS

- Analyzes and extracts information from a biography to answer literal, inferential, and applied questions
- Scans a text to locate specific details
- Compares a character in a text with others and himself/herself
- Makes connections between a text and himself/herself

ANSWER KEY

Literal (Page 46)

1. Fact   2. Fact   3. Opinion   4. Opinion   5. Fact

6. Opinion   7. Opinion (although people debate this to be fact)

Inferential (Page 46)

1. He wasn't part of a cricket team when he was younger and didn't have his own cricket bat and ball. He finally got his first bat at the age of 12.

2. All the years of practice when he was a young child sharpened his reflexes, and he grew to become an exceptional batsman.

3. The English cricket team was not fond of Bradman's success, so much that the English captain Douglas Jardine invented a new type of bowling to try to reduce Bradman's batting score.

Applied (Page 47)

1. Answers will vary. Possible answer(s): proud, accomplished, satisfied, nervous, sense of pride for his country.

2–4. Answers will vary.

Applying Strategies (Page 48)

1.

Year born: 1908	Year died: 2001	Year married: 1932	Year knighted: 1949
Number of runs when awarded first cricket bat: 37		Age Bradman earned his highest number of runs: 21	
Highest number of runs: 452		First overseas tour run score at Leeds: 334	
Years Australia lost the Ashes Tour in England: 1932–1933		Year Donald was captain of national team for first time: 1936	
Length of career as a cricketer: 20 years		Age at death: 92	

2. a–c. Answers will vary.

EXTENSIONS

- Use the Internet to learn more about the game of cricket and understand the rules. Compare it to an American sport.
- Look at the biographies of other elite cricketers on the Internet.
  - Ricky Ponting   - Allan Border   - Adam Gilchrist   - Steve Waugh   - Matthew Hayden
  - Ian Botham   - Graham Gooch   - Sir Richard Hadley   - Imran Khan   - Douglas Jardine

Name _____

Read the biography of a famous cricket player and answer the questions on the following pages.

Full Name: Donald George Bradman
Born: August 27, 1908, Cootamundra, New South Wales, Australia
Died: February 25, 2001, Adelaide, South Australia, Australia
Major Teams: Australia, New South Wales, South Australia
Also Known As: The Don
Batting Style: Right-hand bat
Bowling Style: Leg break

Donald Bradman, the youngest of one brother and three sisters, moved with his family to Bowral, in New South Wales, when he was two. One of Donald's favorite games as a child was a type of backyard cricket. A golf ball was thrown at a wall, and he would try to hit it with a cricket stump. The constant practice sharpened Donald's reflexes and increased his concentration—adding to his already unique and exceptional abilities as a cricketer.

When he was 12, Donald was keeping score at his father's and older brother's cricket game. Fortunately, they were short of a batsman on this day, so Donald was asked to play. He scored 37 runs and was awarded his very first cricket bat.

When Donald was 18, the state selectors invited him to a cricket trial in Sydney. Although they were looking for a bowler, it was a batsman they discovered that day. By the following year, Donald was representing New South Wales in the Sheffield Shield, where he scored 118 runs against South Australia. Bradman was known as the "baby" of the team, and his fans in Melbourne began to call him "The Don."

During a match in 1930, when Bradman was 21, he earned his highest score—452 runs! He also made 1,000 runs for the season. Donald continued with work and cricket commitments as well as finding time to coach hundreds of schoolchildren.

Bradman's first overseas tour in England was the beginning of his immense fame. Scoring 254 runs at Lords and 334 runs at Leeds, Bradman returned to Australia a celebrity.

For many years, Bradman dominated the game of cricket so much so that English captain Douglas Jardine invented a new type of bowling known as "bodyline" to try to reduce Bradman's batting scores. Australia lost the Ashes Tour in the summer of 1932–33, possibly due to this new (and often regarded as dangerous and unsportsmanlike) style of bowling.

Donald married Jessie Menzies in 1932, and shortly after, they moved to South Australia, where Donald became captain of the team and a state selector. In 1936, Donald Bradman led the national team for the first time as their captain.

After World War II, Bradman, who was approaching his forties and had suffered some illnesses, was chosen to be captain of the Australian team, which defeated England 4–0. His cricketing career spanned 20 years, and his batting averages are the goals of many aspiring young cricketers.

Sir Donald Bradman was knighted in 1949, and for the greater part of the rest of the century, continued to be involved in cricket and its administration. He died in February 2001.

SIR DONALD BRADMAN

Literal   Find the answers directly in the text.

Read each sentence. Decide if each statement is a **Fact** or an **Opinion**.

1. Donald Bradman had four siblings.   ☐ Fact ☐ Opinion

2. Hitting a golf ball with a cricket stump improved   ☐ Fact ☐ Opinion
   Donald's reflexes.

3. By the age of 12, Donald was a better cricketer   ☐ Fact ☐ Opinion
   than his older brother.

4. Donald Bradman was born to be a professional   ☐ Fact ☐ Opinion
   cricket player.

5. Donald turned 24 the year he was married.   ☐ Fact ☐ Opinion

6. Donald Bradman preferred living in South Australia   ☐ Fact ☐ Opinion
   to New South Wales.

7. Donald Bradman was the greatest cricketer of the   ☐ Fact ☐ Opinion
   20th century.

Inferential   Think about what the text says.

1. Why didn't Donald use a cricket bat and ball to practice his batting when he was a child?

   _____

   _____

2. Why do you think the state selectors in Sydney chose Donald for a batsman when they were looking
   for a bowler?

   _____

   _____

3. How do you think the English cricket team felt about Donald Bradman's success?

   _____

   _____

Activities

SIR DONALD BRADMAN

Applied   Use what you know about the text and your own experience.

1. Write some words and phrases to describe how you think Donald felt when he was representing his country in the game of cricket for the first time.

   _____

   _____

   _____

2. Do you think it was fair that the English team changed their bowling style to try to prevent Donald's exceptional run rate?

   _____

   _____

   _____

   _____

   _____

3. Sir Donald Bradman is said to be not only one of the world's greatest cricketers, but also one of the world's greatest athletes. His achievements have been compared to those of Pele (soccer), Tiger Woods (golf), and Michael Jordan (basketball). Do you agree?

   _____

   _____

   _____

   _____

4. Had you heard of the sport cricket before? What other sport does it seem similar to?

   _____

   _____

   _____

   _____

SIR DONALD BRADMAN

Scan the text on page 45 to complete
the following activities.

1. Scan the biography about Sir Donald Bradman and write numbers to answer these questions.

Year born:	Year died:	Year married:	Year knighted:
Number of runs when awarded first cricket bat:		Age Bradman earned his highest number of runs:	
Highest number of runs:		First overseas tour run score at Leeds:	
Years Australia lost the Ashes Tour in England:		Year Donald was captain of national team for first time:	
Length of career as a cricketer:		Age at death:	

2. What type of qualities do you think Donald Bradman possessed to be able to achieve such enormous success in his life (for example; perseverance, commitment, etc.)?

a. With a partner, make a list of some of these qualities.

_____

_____

b. Read through the qualities you have listed. Is there a person you admire who also possesses one or more of these qualities?

Name: _____

Qualities: _____

_____

_____

c. Which qualities do you think you share with the late Sir Donald Bradman? Explain why.

Qualities: _____

_____

_____

_____

Genre: Poetry

READING FOCUS

- Analyzes and extracts information from two poems to answer literal, inferential, and applied questions
- Scans for relevant information
- Makes comparisons between two poems
- Makes connections between feelings expressed in a poem and his/her own feelings

---

ANSWER KEY

Literal (Page 51)

1. True   2. True   3. False   4. True   5. True   6. False   7. True

Inferential (Page 51)

1. Answers will vary. Possible answer(s): "veil of fear," "cuts through like a knife," "embarrassment or sneers," "Her nights are filled with tears," etc.

2. joked, rebuked, and praised

3. She was tormented by her shyness but is slowly finding the courage to come out of her shell.

Applied (Page 52)

1. a. it's painful for her to be so shy

    b. starting to come out of her shell

    c. old pictures and the love they have for Granddad help them cherish the memories

2. Answers will vary.

Applying Strategies (Page 53)

1.

	Sonnet	Elegy
Number of lines	14	20
Rhyming pattern	A-B-A-B	A-B-C-B
Feelings expressed by the poet	pain, uncertainty, hope	sadness
Interesting words or phrases used	Answers will vary.	Answers will vary.
Unfamiliar words or phrases used	Answers will vary.	Answers will vary.

2. a–d. Answers will vary.

EXTENSIONS

- Students may be interested in reading *Elegy* by Robert Seymour Bridges, *Elegy Written in a Country Churchyard* by Thomas Gray, or one of Shakespeare's many sonnets.

- Students may feel that writing an elegy helps to express their grief when a pet or relative dies.

Name _____

Read the poems and answer the questions on the following pages.

Sonnet of a Shy Girl

Beneath the well-presented face
Uncertainty is rife.
A veil of fear gives no grace
And cuts through like a knife.
A juggled word, a hasty phrase
Bring embarrassment or sneers.
Silence fills her waking days
Her nights are filled with tears.
A simple word, a smile, a wave
Begins to crack the ice
As she emerges from her cave
And prepares to pay the price.
The years of shyness slip away
Like rain upon the clay.

Elegy for Granddad

The straw hat sits upon the shelf
The snippers click no more
The weeds now choke the velvety petals
Of the plants once stroked and adored.
A stillness fills the garden air
A few bees brave the quiet
The leaves float softly to the ground
As blossoms take to flight.
The boxes will soon be ready to go
The furniture's divided and stacked
No clothes clutter the dresser drawers
No towels hang on the racks.
No laughter echoes through the rooms
No jokes, rebukes, or praise
For Granddad's voice was stilled the day
We laid him in his grave.
The memories are stored away
In frames and in our heart
We never will forget the love
He gave us from the start.

Name _____

Activities

A SONNET AND AN ELEGY

Literal   Find the answers directly in the text.

Read each sentence. Decide if each statement is **True** or **False**.

1. The sonnet states a problem and then resolves it. ☐ True ☐ False

2. The first four lines of the sonnet follows the rhyming pattern A-B-A-B. ☐ True ☐ False

3. The sonnet has sixteen lines. ☐ True ☐ False

4. The first eight lines of the sonnet state the problem. ☐ True ☐ False

5. The final six lines of the sonnet show how the problem was solved. ☐ True ☐ False

6. The elegy is a happy poem about Granddad's life. ☐ True ☐ False

7. This elegy follows the rhyming pattern A-B-C-B. ☐ True ☐ False

Inferential   Think about what the text says.

1. Write words from the sonnet that indicate that being shy was a painful experience for the girl.

_____

_____

2. Name three things from the text that show that the granddad in the elegy was a good granddad.

- _____

- _____

- _____

3. How did the girl in the sonnet feel about her shyness?

_____

_____

_____

©*Teacher Created Resources*   51   *#8249 Comprehending Text*

Name _____

A SONNET AND AN ELEGY

Applied   Use what you know about the text and your own experience.

1. Rewrite the following lines from the poems in your own words to show that you understand their meaning.

    a. A veil of fear gives no grace
    And cuts through like a knife.

    b. Begins to crack the ice

    c. The memories are stored away
    In frames and in our heart

2. What things could you do to help a shy student in your class? What might you say?

A SONNET AND AN ELEGY

Comparing

After reading both poems on page 50, make a comparison between the sonnet and the elegy.

1. Complete the table to show similarities and differences between the sonnet and the elegy.

	Sonnet	Elegy
Number of lines		
Rhyming pattern		
Feelings expressed by the poet		
Interesting words or phrases used		
Unfamiliar words or phrases used		

Making Connections

2. Complete the sentences to relate the poems to your own experiences.

   a. The feeling of sadness expressed in the elegy reminds me of the time when _____

   _____.

   b. After I read the sonnet of the shy girl, I realized that _____

   _____.

   c. Like the shy girl, I sometimes feel frightened or uncertain when _____

   _____.

   d. The person I most admire is _____

   because _____

   _____

   _____.

Unit 10
Mercury and the Workmen

Genre: Fable

Teacher Information

READING FOCUS

- Analyzes and extracts information from a fable to answer literal, inferential, and applied questions
- Uses sensory imaging to write paragraphs from the viewpoints of different characters
- Makes connections between the text characters and others

ANSWER KEY

Literal (Page 56)

1. Answers will vary but should indicate that the ax was the workman's only way to make a living.

2. gold, silver, then the ax that was lost

3. Answers will vary but should indicate that he wanted some good luck for himself or to get rich like the first workman.

4. Answers may vary, but should indicate the fact that Mercury did not give the second man any ax, including his own, because he lied.

Inferential (Page 56)

1. a. True   b. True   c. True   d. True

2. a. Answers will vary. Possible answer(s): Honesty is the best policy.

   b. Mercury's purpose for testing the two workmen was to see who would be honest and not greedy

Applied (Page 57)

1. a–b. Answers will vary.

Applying Strategies (Page 58)

Answers and drawings will vary.

EXTENSIONS

- Students can select and compare a number of short Aesop's fables.
- Students can write a fable to fit a given moral, such as "the most vocal person is not always the one with the best answer," "appearances can be deceptive," "a worker can only do the best work if he/she has the best tools," etc.
- Students can choose a moral for a classmate to write a fable about.

Name _____

Read the fable and answer the questions on the following pages.

A workman was chopping wood near the banks of a river when his ax accidentally fell into the deep water. He was very upset because the ax was his only means of making a living. He sat down on the bank in great distress, crying and cursing.

Mercury appeared and wanted to know why he was so upset. After the workman told him the reason for his distress, Mercury dove into the river and brought up a golden ax.

"Is this ax the one that you accidentally lost in the river?" Mercury asked.

The workman replied that the ax was not his, so Mercury dove into the water again. This time, he brought up an ax made of silver.

"Is this ax the one that you accidentally lost in the river?" he asked.

Again, the workman replied that the ax was not his.

Mercury dove into the water for the third time, and this time returning with the ax that was lost. The workman claimed the ax and was greatly relieved to have his property returned. Mercury, who was very pleased to see how honest the workman was, gave him the gold and silver axes as well.

When the workman returned home, he related his experience to his friends. One of his friends decided to go to the river to try to obtain the same good luck for himself.

He ran to the river and threw his ax into the water in exactly the same place where his friend had lost his ax. He then sat down to cry and moan about his fate.

Mercury appeared to the man and asked why he was so upset. After the man had explained what had happened, Mercury plunged into the river and brought up a gold ax.

"Is this ax the one that you lost in the river?" he asked.

The man exclaimed that it was and seized the ax.

Mercury knew that the man was lying for his own gain, so he immediately took back the gold ax. To make matters worse, he also refused to retrieve the ax that the man had thrown into the water, leaving the man with nothing.

MERCURY AND THE WORKMEN

| **Literal** | Find the answers directly in the text. |

1. The first workman was very upset when his ax fell into the river because _____

_____.

2. Mercury retrieved the three axes from the river in the following order:

_____.

3. The man who threw his ax into the river did so because _____

_____.

4. Because the man claimed an ax that was not his, Mercury _____

_____.

| **Inferential** | Think about what the text says. |

1. Read each sentence. Decide if each statement is **True** or **False**.

    a. The workman who accidentally lost his ax in the river was an honest, hard-working man.   ☐ True   ☐ False

    b. The man who threw his ax in the river was a greedy and dishonest man.   ☐ True   ☐ False

    c. Mercury rewarded the first workman because he was honest.   ☐ True   ☐ False

    d. Mercury punished the second man because he lied to gain wealth for himself.   ☐ True   ☐ False

2. Write full sentences to answer the following questions.

    a. All fables have a moral. What do you think the moral of this fable is?

    _____

    _____

    b. What do you think Mercury's purpose was for testing the two workmen?

    _____

MERCURY AND THE WORKMEN

Applied   Use what you know about the text and your own experience.

1. Give a real-life example that you may have heard on the news or read about in the newspaper for the following:

   a. A person who was rewarded for hard work and honesty

   _____

   _____

   _____

   _____

   _____

   _____

   _____

   b. A person who tried to gain wealth by being dishonest and was punished in some way instead

   _____

   _____

   _____

   _____

   _____

   _____

   _____

MERCURY AND THE WORKMEN

Sensory Imaging

Write a paragraph from the point of view of each character from page 55, including what each can see, smell, hear, and touch. Also include how each is feeling. A space has been left to illustrate the character or the scene. Be concise and make each paragraph different.

First workman

_____

_____

_____

_____

_____

Mercury

_____

_____

_____

_____

_____

Second workman

_____

_____

_____

_____

_____

Genre: Legend

READING FOCUS

- Analyzes and extracts information from a legend to answer literal, inferential, and applied questions
- Uses sensory imaging to consider a text from the main character's point of view
- Makes connections between his/her own senses and what a character from a text might have sensed

ANSWER KEY

Literal (Page 61)

1. a. the mouth of Maui's fish
   b. where Maui put his foot during his struggle with the fish
   c. the anchor of Maui
   d. the fishhook of Maui
   e. the tail of Maui's fish

2. Aotearoa or Land of the Long White Cloud

3. a. 5   b. 3   c. 1   d. 4   e. 2

Inferential (Page 61)

1. Maui had made the land appear to be a long distance away, so they didn't want to row back.

2. a. the   b. of   c. fish   d. anchor   e. canoe   f. fishhook

3. a. Lake Taupo   b. New Plymouth

Applied (Page 62)

1–2. Answers will vary.

Applying Strategies (Page 63)

1–2. Answers will vary.

EXTENSIONS

- Traditional Maori tales can be found at *http://www.maori.org.nz/*. This website also provides a list of books containing Maori legends. Students may also like to view the movie *Whale Rider* for more information on Maori culture.
- Read legends from different native cultures and compare the common themes.

Read the Maori legend and answer the questions on the following pages.

Long ago, the demigod Maui lived in Hawaiki, the Maori ancestral homeland. He had secret magical powers.

One day, Maui's brothers decided to go fishing in their canoe without him. But Maui hid in the bottom of the boat. His brothers were well out to sea before they found him. They wanted to take Maui back to land, but he used his magic to make the land appear much farther away than it actually was. So the brothers let him stay.

Before long, they stopped rowing and the boat was anchored. Maui brought out his magic fishhook, the jaw of his sorcerer grandmother. He tied it to a rope and then dropped it into the water. Soon, Maui felt a powerful tug on the line.

This does not feel like any ordinary fish, he thought.

Maui began pulling on the line. The fish was so strong that Maui had to brace himself and pull with all his might. But after a long struggle, Maui finally pulled up a giant fish. This fish became the north island of New Zealand or *Te Ika a Maui* ("the fish of Maui"). The fish's mouth is Wellington Harbour, and its tail is the Northland Peninsula.

Immediately after he caught the fish, Maui began to pound it with his greenstone club. This created the mountains and valleys of the island. Maui's fishhook became Mahia Peninsula—the *Te Matau a Maui* ("the fishhook of Maui").

The other islands of New Zealand were also created by Maui. The South Island is his canoe—*Te Waka o Maui* ("the canoe of Maui")—and Kaikoura Peninsula is where he placed his foot during his struggle with the fish. Stewart Island, the tiny island below the South Island, is *Te Punga a Maui* ("the anchor of Maui").

It would be many years later that the Maori people would sail the thousands of miles from Hawaiki to live on these islands. They called the country *Aotearoa* ("Land of the Long White Cloud").

New Zealand
(Aotearoa)

THE CREATION OF NEW ZEALAND

Literal   Find the answers directly in the text.

1. What are each of these places known as to the Maori?

    a. Wellington Harbour _____

    b. Kaikoura Peninsula _____

    c. Stewart Island _____

    d. Mahia Peninsula _____

    e. Northland Peninsula _____

2. What is another name for New Zealand? _____

3. Order these events from 1 to 5.

    a. _____ The Maori people migrated to New Zealand.

    b. _____ Maui caught a giant fish.

    c. _____ Maui's brothers discovered Maui in the canoe.

    d. _____ Maui created the mountains of the North Island.

    e. _____ Maui tied his magic fishhook to a rope.

Inferential   Think about what the text says.

1. Why do you think Maui's brothers let him stay in the canoe? _____

    _____

2. What do you think each of these Maori words means in English?

    a. *te* _____   **b.** *a or o* _____

    c. *ika* _____   **d.** *punga* _____

    e. *waka* _____   **f.** *matau* _____

3.   **a.** Which place on the map of New Zealand is most likely where the Maori believe is the giant fish's heart?

    _____

    b. Which place on the map of New Zealand is most likely where the Maori believe is on one of the giant fish's fins?

    _____

THE CREATION OF NEW ZEALAND

Applied   Use what you know about the text and your own experience.

1. Do you think it is important for people to know legends from their native land? Give reasons to support your opinion.

_____

_____

_____

_____

_____

_____

_____

_____

2. Write a legend about how a fictional island was created. Draw a picture of your fictitious island.

_____

_____

_____

_____

_____

_____

_____

_____

_____

_____

THE CREATION OF NEW ZEALAND

Use the text on page 60 to help you complete this activity. This legend does not give us much information about Maui's point of view. What might he have felt, seen, heard, touched, or smelled?

1. For each of these events from the legend, write your impressions of what Maui might have sensed.

Event	Emotions	Sights, Sounds, Smells, or Touch
Maui hides in the canoe.		
Maui is discovered by his brothers.		
Maui makes the land appear far away.		
Maui pulls in the fish.		
Maui pounds the fish, creating mountains and valleys.		

2. Choose one of the events listed above. Rewrite this section of the legend from Maui's point of view. Include all the senses you listed.

_____

_____

_____

_____

_____

Teacher Information

Genre: Mystery

READING FOCUS

- Analyzes and extracts information from a mystery story to answer literal, inferential, and applied questions
- Considers how sensory imaging can be used by authors to set the scene for the reader
- Makes connections to the setting and the characters in a text

ANSWER KEY

Literal (Page 66)

1. Demi left her tent in a hurry, leaving her shoes behind.
2. • Air changes from stale to fresh
   - Floor has more loose pebbles on it
   - Moss appears on walls
   - Shallow stream appears on floor

Inferential (Page 66)

1. Answers will vary. Possible answer(s): curious; eager to join them; she didn't want to miss out on anything.
2. The friends didn't want to spook each other, in fear that one would scream and wake the bats.
3–4. Answers will vary.

Applied (Page 67)

1. Answers will vary. Possible answer(s): camp counselors
2–3. Answers will vary.

Applying Strategies (Page 68)

1. Answers will vary. Possible answer(s):

   See—dark cave, thin stream of light (the moonlight), grin on Ethan's face

   Hear—steps, bats moving, feet kicking pebbles, water sloshing as they walk through

   Smell—musty odor of cave's air, fresher air

   Touch/Feel—rough texture of cave walls, soft and spongy texture of the moss, icy-cold water

   Taste—almost taste the staleness of the air

2. Answers will vary.

EXTENSIONS

- Other mystery stories students may enjoy reading include the following:
  - *The Mennyms* series by Sylvia Waugh
  - *Harriet the Spy* by Louise Fitzhugh
  - The *Hazel Green* series by Odo Hirsch

Name _____

Read the mystery story and answer the questions on the following pages.

They walk single file, heads bowed as if being led to a hanging. The musty odor of the cave's air fills their nostrils and their mouths—they can almost taste its staleness. Every step they take echoes in their ears.

"The cave's getting narrower," announces Ethan.

Occasionally, the sound of something moving is heard from above. Although all three children had come to the conclusion that there were bats hanging upside down, asleep, above their heads, no one had managed to say the words out loud.

"They will be looking for us by now," Demi announces to Ethan and Nat. She wishes over and over that, for once, she hadn't been her normal, pig-headed self and had just let her two friends sneak out of the camp without her.

The sounds beneath their feet change slightly. The trio seem to be moving and kicking stones and pebbles as they walk now.

Nat sniffs the air. "The air smells better—it's fresher!"

Demi jumps suddenly. She has been running her fingertips along the cave walls, almost enjoying its rough texture, until she feels something soft and spongy.

"There's moss on the walls—that means water." Ethan speaks quietly, hoping not to disturb the winged creatures above him. "We're getting closer."

They walk about another few yards when Demi shrieks. The dry cave floor is all of a sudden a shallow stream of icy-cold water. Demi curses under her breath. She thinks back to earlier in the evening when she had spotted Ethan and Nat doing their "secret-agent" routine between the trees and tents. Her fear of missing out on all the fun had made her slip out of her tent in such haste that she had forgotten to grab her shoes.

Ethan blinks a few times to make sure the thin stream of light he can see ahead of him isn't a mirage. The three friends begin walking faster toward the light.

A minute later, Ethan stops dead, causing Nat to collide into him and Demi to squash her nose into Nat's back, making her eyes water. They have reached the end of the cave.

"We've made it!" Ethan announces. The three friends look around them and then look up. The light, coming from a small, circular opening high above them is moonlight.

Ethan bends down, reaching into the freezing water with both hands, searching for something. He brings his hand up to his eyes and inspects its contents. The moonlight reveals a grin spreading quickly across Ethan's face.

"Have you got the bag, Nat?" Ethan asks excitedly. "C'mon! Help me fill it up!"

THE MYSTERY OF THE CAVE

Literal   Find the answers directly in the text.

1. Why is Demi walking through the cave in bare feet?

    _____

2. Explain three ways the cave changes during the story.

    • _____

      _____

    • _____

      _____

      _____

    • _____

      _____

Inferential   Think about what the text says.

1. List some words and phrases to describe how you think Demi felt when she saw her two friends leaving the campgrounds without her.

    _____

    _____

    _____

2. Although the children suspect there are bats above them, why do you think they never mention it aloud?

    _____

    _____

3. Did Ethan and Nat invite Demi on their adventure into the cave? Why do you think this is?

    _____

    _____

    _____

4. Which of the children do you think planned the trip into the cave? _____

THE MYSTERY OF THE CAVE

Applied   Use what you know about the text and your own experience.

1. **"They will be looking for us by now," Demi announces to Ethan and Nat.**

   Who do you think will be looking for the children? _____

   _____

2. What do you think Ethan uncovered on the floor of the cave? _____

   _____

   _____

3. Continue the story from where it left off. Did they encounter any adventures on the way out of the cave?

   _____

   _____

   _____

   _____

   _____

   _____

   _____

   _____

   _____

   _____

   _____

   _____

   _____

   _____

THE MYSTERY OF THE CAVE

Use the text on page 65 to complete the activities. To help readers imagine a clear picture of a setting in a story, authors often use the five senses to describe the scene. This can help readers to enjoy and understand the story better, especially if the setting is a place that is foreign to them.

1. Reread the story. Highlight the sentences or phrases that describe the scene using one of the senses. Record your findings in the boxes in bullet point form.

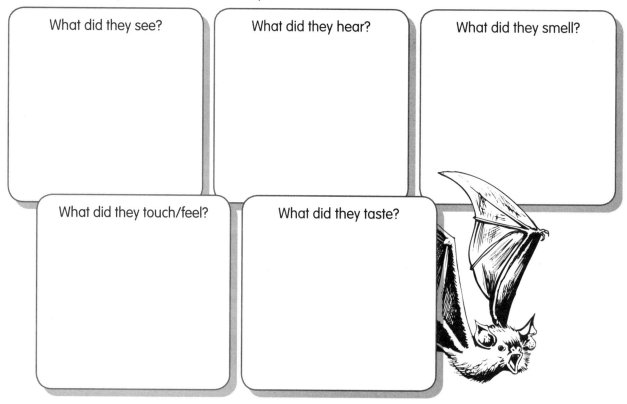

What did they see?

What did they hear?

What did they smell?

What did they touch/feel?

What did they taste?

Making Connections

2. Which character do you think you are the most like: Ethan, the leader; Nat, the quiet follower; or Demi, the friend who doesn't want to be left out?

I am the most like the character _____ *because* _____

_____

_____

_____ .

Unit 13 — First Mission

Genre: Adventure

Teacher Information

READING FOCUS

- Analyzes and extracts information from an adventure narrative to answer literal, inferential, and applied questions
- Uses sensory imaging to describe what he/she imagines the characters and settings of a narrative look like
- Scans a narrative to locate character and setting information

ANSWER KEY

Literal (Page 71)

1. 2:00 p.m.
2. a. He wanted to lose the men.
   b. He wanted to look behind him to see if he was being followed.
   c. He saw the fountain.
   d. He knew the men wouldn't approach him with that many people around.

Inferential (Page 71)

1. It would be easier for him to hide from the enemy.
2. she was telling Sam top secret information

Applied (Page 72)

1–2. Answers will vary.

Applying Strategies (Page 73)

1. **Information Given**
   woman—gypsy
   Sam—unruly hair, heart pounding, spy, first mission
   two men—scruffy looking
   gypsy tent—ornate curtain
   street—small group of people all heading to the fairground
   alleyway—deserted space, leads to the city square
   city square—crowded
   fountain—huge, made of stone

   What I Imagined
   Answers will vary.

2–3. Answers will vary.

EXTENSIONS

- Other adventure stories students may enjoy reading include the following:
  - *Redwall* series by Brian Jacques
  - *The Chronicles of Narnia* by C.S. Lewis
  - *A Series of Unfortunate Events* by Lemony Snicket

FIRST MISSION

Name _____

Read the adventure narrative and answer the questions on the following pages.

Chapter 2

The gypsy woman peered into her crystal ball and sighed deeply.

"I see an unhappy future, young man. You will meet with a tall, dark stranger who will bring peril to your life. He will bear the sign of the rose." She dropped her melodic voice to a whisper. "You must give him the package at the fountain."

Sam nodded and stood up to leave. He felt in his pocket and tossed the woman a coin. "Here."

She caught it and gestured toward the ornate curtain hanging at the back of the tent. "Go out this way, my friend. Good luck."

Sam walked past the woman and pushed the curtain aside. The fairground was crowded, for which he was thankful. He smoothed down his unruly hair and straightened his clothes. Then, his heart pounding, he stalked out.

His first mission as a spy had gone well so far, but now he was reaching the most dangerous part. He knew the enemy was watching. They could be anywhere and look like anyone. Remembering his training, Sam forced himself into a casual stroll as if he were enjoying the sights and sounds of the fair like anyone else. He glanced at his watch. 1:50 p.m. He had to be at the fountain in the next ten minutes to meet his contact. The sign of the rose. What exactly did that mean? He had no idea.

Sam reached the fairground gates and paused. With a sudden, practiced movement, he dropped a handkerchief onto the ground and twisted around to pick it up, taking the chance to scan behind him. Two scruffy-looking men were walking in his direction, staring at him.

Sam gulped, picked up the handkerchief, and continued through the gates. Only a small group of people was in the street up ahead, all heading to the fairground. Sam could hear the men walking behind him. Should he run or play it cool? For a few more seconds, he kept to his slow pace. Then, he exploded into action, charging off down the street.

"Faster, faster!" he urged himself, his feet thundering on the uneven surface.

Up ahead, he spotted an alleyway and darted into it, hoping to lose the men. But it didn't work. He could hear their echoing footsteps growing louder in the deserted space. Panting, Sam wildly looked around for an escape. Then he saw it. Up ahead. The crowded city square, with its huge stone fountain.

Sam felt relief flow into his body. He gradually slowed his pace as he reached the end of the alleyway, knowing the men wouldn't dare attempt to approach him with this many people around. He pushed his way through to the fountain, thinking hard. He still had to find his contact and pass the package to him, all without the men seeing what was going on. He didn't have a clue how he was going to do it.

FIRST MISSION

Literal Find the answers directly in the text.

1. What time did Sam have to be at the fountain? _____

2. Why did Sam:

  a. dart into the alleyway? _____

  _____

  b. drop the handkerchief? _____

  _____

  c. feel relief? _____

  _____

  d. slow down at the end of the alleyway? _____

  _____

Inferential Think about what the text says.

1. Why was Sam thankful that the fairground was crowded?

_____

_____

_____

2. Complete the following sentence.

The gypsy woman dropped her voice to a whisper because _____

_____

_____.

FIRST MISSION

Applied   Use what you know about the text and your own experience.

1. What do you think the "sign of the rose" might mean?

   _____

   _____

   _____

   _____

2. Continue the story of what may happen next.

   Chapter 3

   _____

   _____

   _____

   _____

   _____

   _____

   _____

   _____

   _____

   _____

   _____

   _____

   _____

FIRST MISSION

When we read a narrative, we create images in our minds of the characters and settings. We do this by processing the information that is given in the text and then using our imaginations to build on it.

1. Write any information that was given in the text on page 70 about these characters and settings, and then write what you imagined each one looked like.

	Information Given	What I Imagined
woman		
Sam		
the two men		
gypsy tent		
street		
alleyway		
city square		
fountain		

2. Which image(s) was/were the strongest for you? Why do you think this is?

_____

_____

_____

_____

3. Choose two of your descriptions, and compare them to a partner's. Are they similar? Discuss possible reasons why/why not.

Genre: Persuasive

READING FOCUS

- Analyzes and extracts information from a persuasive advertisement to answer literal, inferential, and applied questions
- Determines the importance of information contained in a text
- Uses synthesis to prepare an interview based on the claims made in a persuasive advertisement

ANSWER KEY

Literal (Page 76)

1. Call the telephone number in the advertisement.
2. You would need to call the telephone number within seven days.
3. It has no added salt, sugar, or fat; it contains no dangerous chemicals; and it has been grown under strictly controlled conditions in pure, clean air.
4. the Rocky Mountains

Inferential (Page 76)

1–2. Answers will vary.

Applied (Page 77)

Answers will vary.

Applying Strategies (Page 78)

1. groundbreaking technology; vegetables taste like junk food; no added salt, sugar, or fat; modified safely; no dangerous chemicals; healthiest and best-tasting vegetables in the world; nearly the same price as regular supermarket vegetables; easy to order

2–5. Answers will vary.

EXTENSIONS

- Ask the students to collect different forms of persuasive writing from newspapers and magazines. These may include letters, articles, editorials, etc.

Name _____

Read the persuasive advertisement and answer the questions on the following pages.

Parents! Can't get your kids to eat their vegetables?

WELL, NOW THERE IS A SOLUTION!

Thanks to groundbreaking technology developed by leading food scientists, you can now enjoy **VEGETABLES THAT TASTE LIKE JUNK FOOD!**

Kids! Do you wish your parents would let you eat junk food all the time?

Incredible but true! Imagine eating

- zucchinis that taste like potato chips
- pumpkins that taste like chocolate
- broccoli that tastes like pizza
- Brussels sprouts that taste like ice cream
- and much more!

Does this sound like a diet disaster? It's not! **Tastyveg** has no added salt, sugar, or fat.

IT IS ONLY THE TASTE THAT HAS BEEN MODIFIED—SAFELY.

No dangerous chemicals have been used. **Tastyveg** has been developed and grown under strictly controlled conditions in the pure, clean air of the Rocky Mountains. Beware of imitations—**Tastyveg** are probably the healthiest and best-tasting vegetables in the world!

Thousands of happy customers are already enjoying the amazing benefits of **Tastyveg**. Here is what they have been saying about this incredible product:

Tastyveg is a safe and easy way to get my kids to eat their vegetables. I can't stop them from eating their Tastyveg! Buying junk food is a thing of the past.

—Ryan Kristiansand

I had been unhealthy for years—I was a junk food addict. That has all changed thanks to Tastyveg. I'm now fit and healthy. This could be you, too! Get your hands on some Tastyveg!

—Katie Oslo

AND NOW IT'S YOUR TURN!

Yes, **Tastyveg** is now available in your area—for a select number of customers. And here is some more good news—**Tastyveg IS NEARLY THE SAME PRICE AS REGULAR SUPERMARKET VEGETABLES!**

It's so easy! Call 1-800-809-2220 to place a weekly vegetable order. If you call within 7 days, you will receive your first order for half price!

Don't delay! Try Tastyveg today!

JUNK-FOOD VEGETABLES

| **Literal** | Find the answers directly in the text. |

1. What do you need to do if you want to buy some **Tastyveg**?

_____

_____

2. How could you get some **Tastyveg** for half the normal price?

_____

_____

3. List the reasons why **Tastyveg** is supposed to be healthy.

_____

_____

_____

4. Where is **Tastyveg** produced? _____

| **Inferential** | Think about what the text says. |

1. Which group do you think this advertisement would most appeal to?

☐ parents   ☐ children   ☐ unhealthy people   ☐ healthy people

Give reasons for your choice. _____

_____

_____

2. A friend of yours reads the advertisement and is eager to buy some **Tastyveg**. Your friend says, "They will be cheap to buy and are the healthiest and best-tasting vegetables in the world!"

Do you agree? Write what you would say to your friend. _____

_____

_____

JUNK-FOOD VEGETABLES

Applied   Use what you know about the text and your own experience.

Imagine you buy some **Tastyveg**, and the product is just as good as it is claimed to be in the advertisement. Would you want to eat vegetables that taste like junk food? Give reasons.

_____

_____

_____

_____

_____

_____

_____

_____

_____

_____

_____

_____

_____

_____

_____

_____

_____

_____

Tastyveg

Name _____

Applying Strategies

JUNK-FOOD VEGETABLES

Determining Importance   Use the text on page 75 to help you complete this activity.

1. Food advertisements like the one for **Tastyveg** often make claims that encourage people to buy the product. List some of the claims of **Tastyveg**.

   _____

   _____

2. Which of the **Tastyveg** claims do you find difficult to believe? Imagine you get the chance to interview a representative from the **Tastyveg** company. Write five questions you would like to ask about the product.

   Synthesizing

   • _____

   • _____

   • _____

   • _____

   • _____

3. Now imagine you are the **Tastyveg** representative. Write answers to your questions, defending the company. You can be as creative as you like!

   • _____
     _____

   • _____
     _____

   • _____
     _____

   • _____
     _____

   • _____
     _____

4. Find a partner. Discuss the questions and answers you wrote, and compare them to your partner's. Choose your five favorite questions and answers. Prepare a television interview, with one of you as the interviewer and the other as the **Tastyveg** representative.

5. When you have practiced your interview, present it to the class.

#8249 Comprehending Text   78   *©Teacher Created Resources*

Teacher Information

Genre: Science Fiction

READING FOCUS

- Analyzes and extracts information from a science-fiction story to answer literal, inferential, and applied questions
- Determines importance by identifying key elements in a story
- Makes predictions about a character
- Makes connections with events in a text and his/her own beliefs

---

ANSWER KEY

Literal (Page 81)

1. False	2. True	3. False	4. True	5. False	6. False

Inferential (Page 81)

1–2. Answers will vary.

3. The dogs stop barking because the green light disappears, and the treehouse looks normal once again.

4. Answers will vary.

Applied (Page 82)

1–3. Answers will vary.

Applying Strategies (Page 83)

1.

Setting	Characters
Ashlea and Krystal's home and the treehouse in the garden	Ashlea, Krystal, twins' mother and father

Main Idea
Twin girls who can read each other's minds go on an adventure inside a treehouse.

Events
The twins sneak out of the house at night to visit the treehouse. The Maltese terriers are barking at the green light coming from the treehouse. The green light disappears. The next day, the twins are on their way to school, when they see their father deep in thought at the base of the treehouse. Ashlea assures Krystal not to worry and states that their father misses the treehouse and wishes he could come with them at night.

Your Opinion of the Story (What did you like/dislike?)
Answers will vary.

2. Answers/drawings will vary.

3. Answers will vary.

EXTENSIONS

- Science-fiction novels students may enjoy reading include the following:
  - *The Watertower* by Gary Crew
  - *The Neverending Story* by Michael Ende
  - *The Lord of the Rings* series by J.R.R. Tolkein

Name _____

Read the science-fiction story and answer the questions on the following pages.

The silence of the still, cloudless night is interrupted by the frantic barking of two Maltese terriers. Twins—Ashlea and Krystal—look up at the window. Smiles appear on their identical faces.

"Time to go!" thinks Ashlea.

The girls slide out of their beds and sneak into the dark corridor. Ashlea reaches for Krystal's hand, and they walk barefoot past their parents' bedroom. The twins overhear a discussion about the noisy dogs. Their father yells in a loud, stern voice for the dogs to be quiet. His wife has decided that large rats must be on the roof, setting the dogs off.

Ashlea opens the back door, knowing it won't be locked. The girls walk by the dogs, who are still barking and snapping their jaws up toward the star-filled sky. They arrive at the base of the largest tree in the garden. They look up—their exotic, almond-shaped eyes twinkle with anticipation.

Ashlea reaches for the first wooden rung of the makeshift ladder. Krystal follows her, climbing up toward their treehouse. Ashlea pauses.

"I AM being careful!" Krystal whispers with a furrowed brow.

The treehouse sits in the branches of the oldest tree in the garden. It was built for their father when he was a little boy, with planks of wood nailed together for the floor, walls, and a ceiling, and an old piece of plaster board acting as a miniature door. The girls love their treehouse because it is the perfect size for them, but its low ceiling means adults only climb up the ladder and peer in—never enter.

The girls reach the top.

Ashlea calls, "We're here."

"Can we come with you?" Krystal asks excitedly. The girls climb inside.

If the twins' mother had opened the bedroom window at that very

moment, and looked toward the treehouse, she would have seen shards of brilliant emerald-green light escaping out of the gaps between the wood planks and from under the door.

As quickly as the green light appears, it is gone. The treehouse becomes a nest of shadows once more. The dogs' barking stops. The cloudless night, once again, is still.

The next morning, the girls are pouring cereal into their bowls, discussing whether they had any homework, when their mother enters the kitchen.

"Goodness! You girls are always so quiet! People will think you don't like each other." Their mother takes the phone from its charger. "I must call someone about the rats on our roof."

Krystal, with a mouth full of cereal, thinks, "They won't find any rats here."

"I know," responds Ashlea, giggling.

"What's so funny?" her mother inquires.

"Nothing, Mother." Ashlea places her bowl in the sink. "We are going to school now."

The twins collect their backpacks and kiss their mother goodbye. They begin the short walk through their garden to the back fence of the school. They look over at their treehouse to see their father standing at its base, deep in thought. Krystal shudders and begins to worry that he might try to stop them from visiting the treehouse at night. She looks over at her older sister . . . waiting.

Creases in Ashlea's forehead appear. She nods and thinks, "Don't worry, Krystal. He's just wishing that he could come to the treehouse with us at night, too. He misses it."

Krystal grins and starts happily skipping toward the school gate.

THE TREEHOUSE

Find the answers directly in the text.

Read each sentence. Decide if each statement is **True** or **False**.

1. The Maltese terriers stop barking after the twins' father yells at them to be quiet.   ☐ True   ☐ False

2. The girls are excited about their nighttime visits to their treehouse.   ☐ True   ☐ False

3. An adult could easily fit through the door of the treehouse.   ☐ True   ☐ False

4. The twins' father played in the treehouse when he was a little boy.   ☐ True   ☐ False

5. The twins' mother worries about their constant arguing.   ☐ True   ☐ False

6. Krystal is older than Ashlea.   ☐ True   ☐ False

Inferential   Think about what the text says.

1. Do you think the twins' father knows what happens after the light appears in the treehouse? Why?

   _____

   _____

2. Do you think the girls have visited the treehouse at night before? Why?

   _____

   _____

3. Why do the dogs eventually stop barking?

   _____

   _____

4. Do you think someone leaves the back door open for the girls at night? If so, who?

   _____

   _____

Name _____

THE TREEHOUSE

Applied   Use what you know about the text and your own experience.

1. Ashlea is the older twin. Do you think she acts as though she is older? Explain.

_____
_____
_____
_____

2. What is so special about the twins in the story?

_____
_____
_____
_____

3. The girls asked whoever was in the treehouse if they could go with them. Where do you think they go and with whom?

_____
_____
_____
_____
_____
_____
_____
_____
_____

THE TREEHOUSE

Determining Importance

After reading the text on page 80, determine the main idea and events in the story.

1. Reread the story. Complete the boxes below by adding notes.

Setting	Characters
Main Idea	
Events	
Your Opinion of the Story (What did you like/dislike?)	

2. Choose one of the characters from the story, and describe him/her. Draw what you believe the character looks like.

_____

_____

_____

_____

3. Is it possible that the twins were visited by an extraterrestrial? Do you believe in extraterrestrials? With a partner, make a list of "for" and "against" points, considering whether extraterrestrials (aliens) really exist.

Extraterrestrials Do Exist	
For	**Against**

Genre: Report

READING FOCUS

- Analyzes and extracts information from a report to answer literal, inferential, and applied questions
- Determines the importance of information contained in a text
- Reduces a text to a summarizing paragraph

ANSWER KEY

Literal (Page 86)

1. It can be determined if a person is obese by calculating his/her Body Mass Index (BMI). This measures the ratio of height to weight. People are considered obese if their BMI is 30 or greater.
2. Children play less sports because it is not offered by many schools. There is also the cost involved in joining a recreational league or a club team, such as membership fees and uniforms, and the time spent on transporting to practice and games.
3. The authors of the report believe that if advertising directed at children focused on promoting a more active lifestyle and eating healthier food options, the occurrences of childhood obesity may decrease.

Inferential (Page 86)

1. Answers will vary. Possible answer(s): Jamie and Hamish were assigned to write the report for Mr. Elliot's class.
2. Answers will vary.

Applied (Page 87)

1–3. Answers will vary.

Applying Strategies (Page 88)

1. a. Answer will vary.

   b.

Main Idea		
the rate of childhood obesity is on the rise		
Possible Cause 1	**Possible Cause 2**	**Possible Cause 3**
spend more time in front of a screen	less sports being offered	advertisements promoting junk food
Other Points	**Possible Solution**	
Answers will vary.	promote a more active lifestyle and healthier food options	

2. Answers will vary.

EXTENSIONS

- In groups, choose one of the following topics and create a survey for a group of students in your school:
  - Time spent watching television vs. time spent being active
  - Nutritional vs. unhealthy foods eaten
  - Availability of organized sports (recreational leagues, club teams, cost, transportation, etc.)
  - Advertising during children's television programs
  - Effects of junk food advertisements on children
  - Childhood obesity: Who's responsible?
  - Effects of obesity on children (for example, depression, bullying, health risks, etc.)

Name _____

Read the report and answer the questions on the following pages.

Health Report: Childhood Obesity   **Due:** Tuesday, April 28
Oval Middle School   **Teacher:** Mr. Elliot

. . . .

A lot of attention in the media lately has been focused on childhood obesity. Children weigh more today compared on average to those living decades ago. The percentage of children who are obese has increased dramatically.

Determining if a child is obese can be calculated by looking at his/her Body Mass Index (BMI), which measures the ratio of height to weight. People are considered obese if their BMI is 30 or greater.

Research shows a number of possible causes contribute to the increase in children's weight.

Children today spend more time in front of a screen compared to those of 30 years ago. Children watch television and play computer games instead of playing outside. We conducted a survey of 50 children from the ages of 6 to 14 that showed, on average, children are spending four hours a day in front of a screen.

Another factor that is possibly affecting children's weight is that many schools today do not offer extracurricular sports outside of school hours. For children to play sports, they have to join a recreational league or a club team, which costs money and time. Factors such as the cost of membership and uniforms, and the time spent on transporting the children to practice and games, may be some of the reasons why children are less likely to join organized sports. Our survey of 50 children showed the following:

- 22 children participated in an organized sport.

- 15 children would participate in an organized sport if there was less cost involved.

- 13 children would not like to play a sport outside of school hours.

Another possible reason why children weigh more today than they did 30 years ago involves advertising of snack food and junk food. If children are watching approximately four hours of television each day, this means they are being exposed to many junk food and fast food commercials. Children may then pressure their parents to purchase food with little or no nutritional value.

Some large companies use children's favorite cartoon characters or actors to promote their products and even include toys with their meals. Our survey showed that 33 out of 50 children ask their parents to buy fast food because they want the toy included with the meal.

The rate of childhood obesity is increasing. Possible reasons include: children being less active and spending too much time in front of screens, less sports being offered in schools, and junk food advertising that is directed at children. If advertising for children promoted having a more active lifestyle and healthier food options, we believe that the occurrences of childhood obesity may decrease.

Written by Jamie M. and Hamish C.

CHILDHOOD OBESITY

> **Literal**   Find the answers directly in the text.

1. How is it determined whether a person is obese? _____

_____

_____

2. Give reasons why children are playing less sports.

_____

_____

_____

3. What do the authors of the report believe will help to improve the problem of childhood obesity?

_____

_____

_____

> **Inferential**   Think about what the text says.

1. Why did Jamie and Hamish most likely write the report?

_____

_____

_____

2. How do you think Jamie and Hamish collected their statistics for their report?

_____

_____

_____

CHILDHOOD OBESITY

Applied   Use what you know about the text and your own experience.

1. If you surveyed children in your school about how they spent their time and their eating habits, do you think you would have results similar to those in the report? Explain your answer.

_____

_____

2. Do you think fast food companies should be allowed to include children's toys with their meals? Why or why not?

_____

_____

3. Write a report promoting a healthier lifestyle. What are some things you can incorporate into your life to improve your health?

_____

_____

_____

_____

_____

_____

_____

_____

_____

_____

_____

_____

_____

_____

Name _____

CHILDHOOD OBESITY

Use the text on page 85 to complete the activities. Being able to identify keywords and phrases in a text and then summarizing that information are important skills to learn—and they take practice!

1. The principal at Oval Middle School is so impressed with Jamie and Hamish's report that he has asked you to summarize the report into one paragraph for the school newsletter.

   a. Reread the text. Underline keywords and phrases.

   b. Sort the words and phrases you have underlined by placing them into one of the following categories.

Main Idea		
Possible Cause 1	Possible Cause 2	Possible Cause 3
Other Points		Possible Solution

2. Use the information above to write one paragraph that summarizes the report about childhood obesity.

_____

_____

_____

_____

_____

_____

_____

_____

Genre: Review

READING FOCUS

- Analyzes and extracts information from a movie review to answer literal, inferential, and applied questions
- Scans a movie review to locate and identify the writer's opinions
- Compares and analyzes differing opinions and aspects of a review

ANSWER KEY

Literal (Page 91)

1. She thought they were both skilled at using facial expressions.
2. *Chase* and *Crime Scene*
3. Nathan Clark
4. adventure
5. Ruth Kinmont

Inferential (Page 91)

1–2. Answers will vary.

Applied (Page 92)

1–2. Answers will vary.

3. Drawings will vary.

Applying Strategies (Page 93)

1. The list of likes and dislikes should be similar to the following:

Likes	Dislikes
The actors use good facial expression.	There is too much focus on the action scenes and not enough on the characters' personal growth.
The cinematography is breathtaking and makes you feel as though you are sharing in the adventure.	The script is poor, particularly the conversations between Zac and Mason.
The movie is entertaining and colorful.	The music is boring and dreary.
The movie will keep young viewers on the edge of their seats.	The movie is too long; several scenes could have been cut.

2. a–b. Answers will vary.

EXTENSIONS

- Weekend newspapers and the Internet are excellent sources of movie reviews. The students can compare the styles used in different sources.
- Students can write their own review about a recent book they have read or movie they have seen.

BEACH HOTEL

Name _____

Read the movie review and answer the questions on the following pages.

Beach Hotel (rated PG)

Starring Foster Adams and Nathan Clark   Directed by Candace Marsh

Rating: ★ ★ ★

Based on the popular children's novel by Ruth Kinmont, this movie has been eagerly anticipated by thousands of pre-teens.

The plot is simple—11-year-old Zac and his best friend Mason go to the beach where they decide to investigate an old, deserted hotel. Soon afterward, a stranger appears, warning them to stay away. The boys don't take any notice and soon find themselves embroiled in a hair-raising adventure.

Making their movie debuts, Foster Adams (Zac) and Nathan Clark (Mason) are appealing to watch. They are both skilled at using facial expressions to show their emotions as they embark on a whirlwind journey through twisting tunnels, spooky forests, and rocky clifftops. The cinematography is breathtaking and makes you feel as if you are sharing in the adventure along with the two main characters.

But while the movie is certainly visually exciting, fans of the novel might be disappointed with the way Zac and Kieran are portrayed on the big screen. Director Candace Marsh (*Chase* and *Crime Scene*) has concentrated too much on the action scenes and glosses over the personal growth of the characters as they face their worst fears.

The script and the music in the movie are also a letdown. It is baffling that the scriptwriters chose to avoid any tension-filled conversations between the main characters from the novel. Instead, Zac and Mason say things of little importance to each other. The background music is boring and dreary—something brighter would have been more appropriate for an adventure movie.

Beach Hotel is surprisingly long for a movie aimed at children (running at close to three hours), and you leave the theater with the feeling that several scenes could have been cut, particularly the first scene showing the car trip to the beach.

However, *Beach Hotel* will certainly keep its young viewers on the edge of their seats. It is an entertaining and colorful ride and is certain to be a winner.

—Jody Flynn

BEACH HOTEL

Literal   Find the answers directly in the text.

1. What did the reviewer like about the actors who played the main characters?

   _____

   _____

2. Name two other movies directed by Candace Marsh.

   _____ and _____

3. Which actor played the role of Mason?

   _____

4. What is the genre of the movie?

   _____

5. Who wrote the novel *Beach Hotel*?

   _____

Inferential   Think about what the text says.

1. Summarize the plot of *Beach Hotel* in one or two sentences.

   _____

   _____

   _____

   _____

   _____

2. Based on your summary, suggest an alternative title for the movie.

   _____

   _____

BEACH HOTEL

Applied Use what you know about the text and your own experience.

1. Imagine you are an entertainment reporter. You are asked to interview director Candace Marsh about the movie. Write three questions you would like to ask her.

   • _____

     _____

   • _____

     _____

   • _____

     _____

2. Circle one of your questions. Write what you think Candace's answer might be.

   _____

   _____

   _____

3. In the space below, create a flyer to promote the movie.

BEACH HOTEL

A movie review contains the writer's opinions on different aspects of the movie.

1. Scan the movie review on page 90 to list reviewer Jody Flynn's likes and dislikes of *Beach Hotel*.

Likes	Dislikes
_____	_____
_____	_____
_____	_____
_____	_____
_____	_____
_____	_____

2. Imagine you are a movie reviewer. You go to see *Beach Hotel* but find that your opinions are very different from Jody Flynn's! In fact, everything Flynn liked about the movie, you disliked. Everything she disliked, you liked.

Comparing

a. Highlight two of Flynn's likes. Rewrite them as dislikes. For example, "The costumes were bright and colorful," could become, "The costumes were gaudy and overdone."

- _____
  _____

- _____
  _____

b. Highlight two of Flynn's dislikes. Rewrite them as likes. For example, "The actors mumbled and were difficult to understand," could become, "The voices of the actors were soft and subtle and drew you into the movie."

- _____
  _____

- _____
  _____

Genre: Informational Text— Timetable

READING FOCUS

- Analyzes and extracts information from a bus timetable to answer literal, inferential, and applied questions
- Scans text to locate specific information
- Synthesizes a range of information to plan a bus timetable to fulfill a number of different criteria

---

ANSWER KEY

Literal (Page 96)

1. c
2. d
3. a
4. 9:05 a.m.

Inferential (Page 96)

1. 7:13, 8:13, and 8:58
2. Answers will vary. Possible answer(s): to transport people going to work in the morning.

Applied (Page 97)

1. Answers will vary.
2. Answers will vary. Possible answer(s):

    Advantages—set schedule, saves on gas money, inexpensive, better for the environment

    Disadvantages—availability of times can be limited, location of stations could be far from your home or your destination

3. a. Answers will vary. Possible answer(s): good form of exercise, fresh air.

    b. Answers will vary. Possible answer(s): safety when crossing a busy intersection, weather, distance to get to school.

Applying Strategies (Page 98)

1–2. Answers will vary.

EXTENSIONS

- Collect examples of timetables, and compare the different formats, depending on what it is for (e.g., transportation, TV programs).
- Students can conduct a survey and graph the results, showing how class members travel to school.

BUS TIMETABLE

Name _____

Read the bus timetable and answer the questions on the following pages.

Bus to Trent

E = Express

Brighton Station	Sandy Beach	Fishing Bay	Twin Rocks	Trent Station
6:40 a.m. (E)				7:10
7:05	7:13		7:29	7:39
7:40 (E)				8:10
8:05	8:13	8:25		8:39
8:20 (E)				8:50
8:50	8:58	9:10	9:15	9:25
9:15			9:38	9:48
9:40	9:48	10:00	10:05	10:15
10:20	10:25			10:58
11:05	11:13	11:25	11:30	11:40
11:40		11:59		12:13 p.m.

Bus to Brighton

E = Express

Trent Station	Twin Rocks	Fishing Bay	Sandy Beach	Brighton Station
6:30 a.m. (E)				7:00
7:00 (E)				7:30
7:25 (E)				7:55
8:05	8:15			8:38
8:30	8:40	8:45	8:57	9:05
9:00	9:10	9:15	9:27	9:35
9:20		9:34		9:53
9:50	10:00	10:05	10:17	10:25
10:25	10:35		10:51	10:59
11:00	11:10	11:15	11:27	11:35
11:35	11:45	11:50	12:02	12:10 p.m.

BUS TIMETABLE

Literal   Find the answers directly in the text.

Select the correct answer.

1. The 9:20 bus from Trent station . . .

   a. ☐ stops at Sandy Beach.   b. ☐ is an express.

   c. ☐ stops at Fishing Bay.   d. ☐ arrives at 9:52.

2. The bus that arrives at Trent at 11:40 . . .

   a. ☐ stops at two places.   b. ☐ leaves Brighton at 11:35.

   c. ☐ takes 30 minutes.   d. ☐ stops at Twin Rocks.

3. The express buses . . .

   a. ☐ provide a nonstop service.   b. ☐ arrive before 8:30.

   c. ☐ only run before 8:00 in   d. ☐ stop at Sandy Beach.
        the morning.

4. When is the earliest a person leaving Sandy Beach could arrive by bus in Brighton?

   _____

Inferential   Think about what the text says.

1. At what times could a person leaving Sandy Beach catch the bus to make it to Trent no later than 9:30 a.m.?

   _____

2. Why do you think the express buses run at the times they do?

   _____

   _____

BUS TIMETABLE

Applied   Use what you know about the text and your own experience.

1. Which times do you think the express buses would be likely to run in the afternoon? Why?

   _____

   _____

   _____

   _____

2. List some of the advantages and disadvantages of public transportation.

Advantages	**Disadvantages**
_____	_____
_____	_____
_____	_____
_____	_____
_____	_____

3.   **a.** Write two advantages of students walking to school.

   • _____

   _____

   • _____

   _____

   b. Write two disadvantages or concerns regarding students walking to school.

   • _____

   _____

   • _____

   _____

BUS TIMETABLE

Synthesizing

1. Prepare a bus timetable for travel from the city you live in to a destination of your choice. Have three possible stops along the way before the final destination.

Bus Timetable

From: _____   To: _____

Starting Station	Stop 1	Stop 2	Stop 3	Final Destination

2. **a.** Write three questions to ask a classmate about your bus timetable.

   • _____

   • _____

   • _____

   b. Pair up with a classmate and take turns answering each other's questions.

Genre: Humor

READING FOCUS

- Analyzes and extracts information from a humorous narrative to answer literal, inferential, and applied questions
- Writes character and plot summaries of a humorous narrative
- Predicts events that may take place after the close of a narrative

ANSWER KEY

Literal (Page 101)

1. She was looking out the window, daydreaming.

2. b, c, and d

Inferential (Page 101)

1. Answers will vary but should mention that Holly blushed and looked at her shoes when she talked to Justin.

2. Answers will vary. Possible answer(s): embarrassed, mortified, humiliated.

3. Stacy had stated, "You didn't hear any of that, did you?" and Miss Turner stated, "Maybe it might finally teach her to pay attention."

Applied (Page 102)

1–2. Answers will vary.

Applying Strategies (Page 103)

1. Answers will vary, but may include some of the following:

   - Holly reads the words on the board.
   - Holly tries to remember the story.
   - Holly writes a love letter.
   - Holly gives what she thinks is the permission slip to Justin.
   - Holly puts Justin's letter, and what she thinks is her letter, on Miss Turner's desk.
   - The bell rings, and Holly leaves the classroom.
   - Miss Turner calls out to Holly.
   - Holly sees Justin and his friends with her letter.

2–3. Answers will vary.

EXTENSIONS

- Other humorous books students may enjoy include the following:
  - *Paul Jennings' Funniest Stories* by Paul Jennings
  - *The Giraffe and the Pelly and Me* by Roald Dahl
  - *The 26-Story Treehouse* by Andy Griffiths

PAY ATTENTION

Name _____

Read the humorous narrative and answer the questions on the following pages.

"Okay, class. Now that you've listened carefully to the story, you may begin the activity on the board."

Uh-oh. I whipped my head away from the window. Miss Turner's voice had interrupted my daydream.

Stacey was frowning at me. "You didn't hear any of that, did you?"

I shook my head and read the words on the board with a sinking feeling in my stomach. *Write a letter from one of the characters that describes his or her feelings.* I turned to Stacey in panic. She rolled her eyes and started to speak.

"Stacey, no talking!" Miss Turner snapped. "This is a test. If Holly wasn't listening, that's her fault. Maybe it will finally teach her to pay attention." Miss Turner folded her arms and glared at me.

I groaned and massaged my temples. Had any of the story filtered through my brain? Hmm . . . there had been something about a princess who secretly loved a poor man . . . she was trying to organize a way to meet him at the palace gates. It was typical of the sappy stuff Miss Turner was always reading to us.

I picked up my pencil. It was simple. I'd write a love letter from the princess to the poor man. I'd make it as flowery as I could, and Miss Turner would be sure to like it.

I wrote, *You are the man of my dreams. My heart beats quickly whenever you are near.* That was a good start. I added some more mushy phrases and finished with, *Meet me at the gates at 3 p.m.* Then I drew lots of love hearts and kisses. I looked at my letter admiringly. There. Miss Turner would have to be happy with that. It hadn't mattered that I hadn't been paying attention.

"Class, when you've finished, please bring your letters to my desk. Oh, and if anyone hasn't handed in the permission slip for next week's field trip, please give it to Justin."

Justin was the notes monitor for the week. He was also the best-looking boy in the class. I scooped up my letter and my permission slip and went to his desk first.

"Here," I said, not looking at him. I felt my cheeks flame as I held out the form.

"Er, thanks. Can you hand my letter to Miss Turner?" he asked.

"Okay," I said, looking at my shoes. I grabbed his letter and put it on Miss Turner's desk with mine. Then I went back to my seat.

A few minutes later, the bell rang. I breathed a sigh of relief. Three o'clock was the best part of the school day. I picked up my bag, waited for Stacey, and then started to walk to the school gates to meet my little brother.

"Holly!" I spun around. Miss Turner was walking toward me. "Where is your letter? You handed me your permission slip by mistake."

"But I gave that to . . ." I started. Then it hit me. I gulped and looked toward the gates. Justin was standing there with three of his friends, my love letter in his hand.

"Holly loves Justin." I could just hear the singing over the snickers and giggles.

Maybe today would be the day I'd finally learn to pay attention.

PAY ATTENTION

Find the answers directly in the text.

1. Why didn't Holly hear any of Miss Turner's story?

_____

_____

_____

2. Mark an **X** next to the statements Holly would agree with.

    a. ☐ The end of the school day is the worst part of going to school.

    b. ☐ Miss Turner likes sappy stories.

    c. ☐ Justin is good-looking.

    d. ☐ The love letter was well written.

Think about what the text says.

1. How do you think Holly felt about speaking to Justin? Explain why you think this.

_____

_____

_____

2. List words to describe how you think Holly felt at the end of the story.

_____

_____

3. What evidence in the text proves that this was not the first time Holly wasn't paying attention?

_____

_____

_____

PAY ATTENTION

Applied   Use what you know about the text and your own experience.

1. Imagine you are Miss Turner. Complete comments on this school report card for Holly.

Holly's Report Card

Writing

_____
_____
_____
_____

Listening

_____
_____
_____
_____

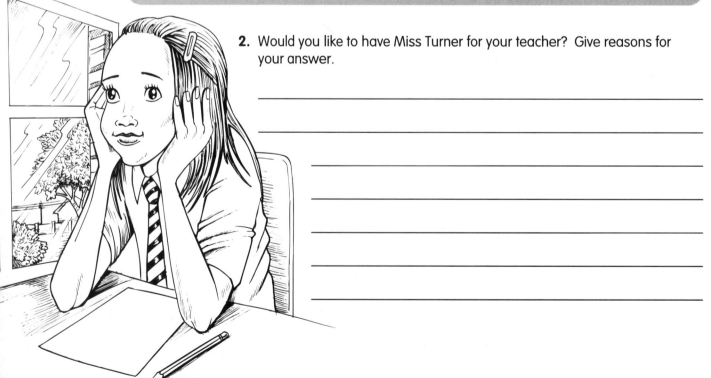

2. Would you like to have Miss Turner for your teacher? Give reasons for your answer.

_____
_____
_____
_____
_____
_____

PAY ATTENTION

Summarizing

Use the text on page 100 to help you complete this activity.

1. Summarize the plot of the story by listing the main events in the order in which they happen. You should list between six and ten events. The first one has been done for you.

    1. Holly realizes that Miss Turner is speaking.

    2. _____

    3. _____

    4. _____

    5. _____

    6. _____

    7. _____

    8. _____

    9. _____

   10. _____

2. Write two or three sentences describing Holly.

_____

_____

_____

3. Based on your plot and character summaries, what do you think Holly might do next after the story ends? Describe six events you would like to see happen.

Predicting

- _____

- _____

- _____

- _____

- _____

- _____

Genre: Play

READING FOCUS

- Analyzes and extracts information from a play to answer literal, inferential, and applied questions
- Summarizes the main events in a play

ANSWER KEY

Literal (Page 106)

1. His tourist guide book.

2. glare, stare at him with open dislike

3. He questions the tour guide about the number of people attending the tour. There should only be 10, but there are 11.

Inferential (Page 106)

1. They are glad to be rid of Mr. Dingles and find it amusing that the tour guide locked him in the restroom.

2. Answers will vary. Possible answer(s): peculiar, literal, disruptive, rude.

3. a. Drawing should depict a happy, pleasant demeanor.

   b. Drawing should depict a mischievous demeanor.

Applied (Page 107)

Answers will vary.

Applying Strategies (Page 108)

1.

Setting Castle's Chocolate Factory	**How does the play begin?** The tour guide begins the tour, and Mr. Dingles questions her regarding the number of people allowed on the tour.
Characters tour guide, Mr. Dingles, tour group	
Main Character Descriptions Mr. Dingles, nose buried in book, peculiar, constantly disrupting and correcting the tour guide	**What happens in the middle?** Mr. Dingles continues to be disruptive and is inconsiderate to the group.
	What happens at the end? The tour guide locks Mr. Dingles in the restroom, and the people in the tour group smile.

2. Answers will vary.

EXTENSIONS

- Look for plays adapted from popular children's books. Some suggested titles include the following:
  - *Charlie and the Chocolate Factory* by Roald Dahl
  - *Charlotte's Web* by E.B. White
  - *Hating Alison Ashley* by Robin Klein
  - *The Lion, the Witch and the Wardrobe* by C.S. Lewis

THE EXPERT

Name _____

Read the play and answer the questions on the following pages.

(A group of 11 people are standing center stage. All are talking quietly, except for one man, Mr. Dingles, who is reading a book. A tour guide walks up to them.)

Tour Guide   Hello and welcome to this tour of the Castle's Chocolate Factory.

Mr. Dingles   *(pushing to the front and waving the book)* Excuse me, Miss. Reg Dingles is my name. According to my trusty tourist guide, there should be a maximum of 10 people on this tour, but I've counted 11.

Tour Guide   That's okay, sir. One extra person won't matter.

(She smiles, but Mr. Dingles wags his finger at her and shakes his head. The tour guide's smile starts to tighten. She motions the group forward a few paces.)

Tour Guide   *(pointing to her right)* Here we are at the wrapping room. Every chocolate we make is wrapped in here.

Mr. Dingles   *(referring to his book)* That's not entirely correct. Castle's Easter eggs are made in your factory in Pine River.

Tour Guide   *(gritting her teeth)* On to another topic . . . Does anyone know what our most popular chocolate is?

(Several people in the group put up their hands, but Mr. Dingles ignores them.)

Mr. Dingles   That would be the Castle's chocolate cat.

(The people who had their hands up glare at him. Mr. Dingles doesn't seem to notice. He goes back to reading his book.)

Tour Guide   Alfred Castle was only 25 when he established this factory . . .

Mr. Dingles   *(with his nose in the book)* 25½ to be exact.

Tour Guide   He became a millionaire . . .

Mr. Dingles   *(still looking at his book)* Billionaire, actually.

(The whole group is now staring at Mr. Dingles with open dislike. The tour guide pauses and then points to a door to her left.)

Tour Guide   To my left, ladies and gentlemen, are our mixing rooms.

Mr. Dingles   Not according to the floor plan in my book.

Tour Guide   Really, sir?

Mr. Dingles   Yes. *(He opens the door and walks in.)* You see, this used to be the mixing area but as of five years ago, it became a restroom.

Tour Guide   You're absolutely correct. *(She shuts the door and locks it.)*

Mr. Dingles   *(in a muffled voice)* Hey, let me out!

Tour Guide   Before we move on, I'll just do a quick head count. *(She mimes counting the group.)* 10. That must be correct. That's the maximum number allowed in a group. *(She smiles.)*

(The group smiles back and follows her offstage. Mr. Dingles's cries fade out.)

THE EXPERT

| **Literal** | Find the answers directly in the text. |

1. Where is Mr. Dingles getting his facts from? _____

_____

2. List two ways the people in the tour group look at Mr. Dingles.

• _____

• _____

3. What's the first thing Mr. Dingles questions the tour guide about?

_____

| **Inferential** | Think about what the text says. |

1. Why does the tour group smile at the end of the play?

_____

_____

2. List words to describe the character of Mr. Dingles.

_____

_____

3. Draw how the tour guide's face might look as she says each of these lines.

a. "Hello and welcome to this tour of the Castle's chocolate factory."	**b.** "You're absolutely correct."

THE EXPERT

Applied   Use what you know about the text and your own experience.

Imagine you are the tour guide. Think of three reasons why you locked Mr. Dingles in the restroom. Now imagine you are Mr. Dingles. Think of three reasons why you did not deserve to be locked in the restroom. Write the reasons below.

Tour Guide

- _____
  _____
  _____

- _____
  _____
  _____

- _____
  _____
  _____

Mr. Dingles

- _____
  _____
  _____

- _____
  _____
  _____

- _____
  _____
  _____

THE EXPERT

After reading the play on page 105, complete the story map to help you create a summary.

1. Complete the story map about the play on page 105.

Setting	How does the play begin?
Characters	
Main Character Descriptions	What happens in the middle?
	What happens at the end?

2. Imagine one member of the tour group calls the local newspaper to describe the events that take place in the play. She gives an accurate summary of what happened. Use your notes to write what the tour group member might say.

_____

_____

_____

_____

_____

_____

_____

Common Core State Standards

Standards Correlations

Each lesson meets one or more of the following Common Core State Standards © Copyright 2010. National Governors Association Center for Best Practices and Council of Chief State School Officers. All rights reserved. For more information about the Common Core State Standards, go to *http://www.corestandards.org/* or *http://www.teachercreated.com/standards*.

Reading Literature/Fiction Text Standards	Text Title	Pages
Key Ideas and Details		
ELA.RL.6.1 Cite textual evidence to support analysis of what the text says explicitly as well as inferences drawn from the text.	Water World The Golden Fish Princess Bella and the Frog Prince Petrified Wood A Sonnet and an Elegy Mercury and the Workmen The Creation of New Zealand The Mystery of the Cave First Mission The Treehouse Pay Attention The Expert	9–13 19–23 24–28 29–33 49–53 54–58 59–63 64–68 69–73 79–83 99–103 104–108
ELA.RL.6.2 Determine a theme or central idea of a text and how it is conveyed through particular details; provide a summary of the text distinct from personal opinions or judgments.	Water World The Golden Fish Princess Bella and the Frog Prince A Sonnet and an Elegy Mercury and the Workmen The Creation of New Zealand The Mystery of the Cave The Treehouse Pay Attention The Expert	9–13 19–23 24–28 49–53 54–58 59–63 64–68 79–83 99–103 104–108
ELA.RL.6.3 Describe how a particular story's or drama's plot unfolds in a series of episodes as well as how the characters respond or change as the plot moves toward a resolution.	The Golden Fish Mercury and the Workmen The Creation of New Zealand The Mystery of the Cave The Treehouse Pay Attention	19–23 54–58 59–63 64–68 79–83 99–103

Common Core State Standards (cont.)

Reading Literature/Fiction Text Standards (cont.)	Text Title	Pages
Craft and Structure		
ELA.RL.6.4 Determine the meaning of words and phrases as they are used in a text, including figurative and connotative meanings; analyze the impact of a specific word choice on meaning and tone.	The Golden Fish Petrified Wood A Sonnet and an Elegy The Creation of New Zealand The Mystery of the Cave First Mission Pay Attention	19–23 29–33 49–53 59–63 64–68 69–73 99–103
ELA.RL.6.5 Analyze how a particular sentence, chapter, scene, or stanza fits into the overall structure of a text and contributes to the development of the theme, setting, or plot.	Water World The Golden Fish A Sonnet and an Elegy The Creation of New Zealand The Mystery of the Cave First Mission Pay Attention The Expert	9–13 19–23 49–53 59–63 64–68 69–73 99–103 104–108
ELA.RL.6.6 Explain how an author develops the point of view of the narrator or speaker in a text.	Mercury and the Workmen The Creation of New Zealand Pay Attention	54–58 59–63 99–103
Integration of Knowledge and Ideas		
ELA.RL.6.9 Compare and contrast texts in different forms or genres (e.g., stories and poems; historical novels and fantasy stories) in terms of their approaches to similar themes and topics.	The Golden Fish Princess Bella and the Frog Prince A Sonnet and an Elegy	19–23 24–28 49–53
Range of Reading and Level of Text Complexity		
ELA.RL.6.10 By the end of the year, read and comprehend literature, including stories, dramas, and poems, in the grades 6–8 text complexity band proficiently, with scaffolding as needed at the high end of the range.	Water World The Golden Fish Princess Bella and the Frog Prince Petrified Wood A Sonnet and an Elegy Mercury and the Workmen The Creation of New Zealand The Mystery of the Cave First Mission The Treehouse Pay Attention The Expert	9–13 19–23 24–28 29–33 49–53 54–58 59–63 64–68 69–73 79–83 99–103 104–108

Reading Informational Text/Nonfiction Standards	Text Title	Pages
Key Ideas and Details		
ELA.RI.6.1 Cite textual evidence to support analysis of what the text says explicitly as well as inferences drawn from the text.	The Rocket Builder Braille Lone Survivor! Sir Donald Bradman Junk–Food Vegetables Childhood Obesity Beach Hotel Bus Timetable	14–18 34–38 39–43 44–48 74–78 84–88 89–93 94–98
ELA.RI.6.2 Determine a central idea of a text and how it is conveyed through particular details; provide a summary of the text distinct from personal opinions or judgments.	The Rocket Builder Lone Survivor! Sir Donald Bradman Childhood Obesity Beach Hotel	14–18 39–43 44–48 84–88 89–93
ELA.RI.6.3 Analyze in detail how a key individual, event, or idea is introduced, illustrated, and elaborated in a text (e.g., through examples or anecdotes).	Sir Donald Bradman Junk–Food Vegetables Childhood Obesity Beach Hotel	44–48 74–78 84–88 89–93
Craft and Structure		
ELA.RI.6.4 Determine the meaning of words and phrases as they are used in a text, including figurative, connotative, and technical meanings.	Braille Lone Survivor! Sir Donald Bradman Childhood Obesity	34–38 39–43 44–48 84–88
ELA.RI.6.5 Analyze how a particular sentence, paragraph, chapter, or section fits into the overall structure of a text and contributes to the development of the ideas.	The Rocket Builder Braille Lone Survivor! Childhood Obesity Beach Hotel	14–18 34–38 39–43 84–88 89–93
ELA.RI.6.6 Determine an author's point of view or purpose in a text and explain how it is conveyed in the text.	The Rocket Builder Braille Lone Survivor! Sir Donald Bradman Childhood Obesity Beach Hotel	14–18 34–38 39–43 44–48 84–88 89–93

Reading Informational Text/Nonfiction Standards *(cont.)*	Text Title	Pages
Integration of Knowledge and Ideas		
ELA.RI.6.7 Integrate information presented in different media or formats (e.g., visually, quantitatively) as well as in words to develop a coherent understanding of a topic or issue.	Junk–Food Vegetables Bus Timetable	74–78 94–98
ELA.RI.6.8 Trace and evaluate the argument and specific claims in a text, distinguishing claims that are supported by reasons and evidence from claims that are not.	Braille Junk–Food Vegetables	34–38 74–78
Range of Reading and Level of Text Complexity		
ELA.RI.6.10 By the end of the year, read and comprehend literary nonfiction in the grades 6–8 text complexity band proficiently, with scaffolding as needed at the high end of the range.	The Rocket Builder Braille Lone Survivor! Sir Donald Bradman Junk–Food Vegetables Childhood Obesity Beach Hotel Bus Timetable	14–18 34–38 39–43 44–48 74–78 84–88 89–93 94–98